"Surrounded by Dangers of All Kinds"

The Mexican War Letters of Lieutenant Theodore Laidley

War and the Southwest Series

Series editors:
Richard G. Lowe, Gustav L. Seligmann, Calvin L. Christman

The University of North Texas Press has undertaken to publish a series of significant books about War and the Southwest. This broad category includes first-hand accounts of military experiences by men and women of the Southwest, histories of warfare involving the people of the Southwest, and analyses of military life in the Southwest itself. The Southwest is defined loosely as those states of the United States west of the Mississippi River and south of a line from San Francisco to St. Louis as well as the borderlands straddling the Mexico-United States boundary. The series will include works involving military life in peacetime in addition to books on warfare itself. It will range chronologically from the first contact between indigenous tribes and Europeans to the present. The series is based on the belief that warfare is an important if unfortunate fact of life in human history and that understanding war is a requirement for a full understanding of the American past.

Books in the series

FOO—A Japanese-American Prisoner of the Rising Sun
Wen Bon: A Naval Air Intelligence Officer behind Japanese Lines in China
An Artist at War: The Journal of John Gaitha Browning
The 56th Evac Hospital: Letters of a WWII Army Doctor
CAP Môt: The Story of a Marine Special Forces Unit in Vietnam, 1968–1969

"Surrounded by Dangers of All Kinds"

The Mexican War Letters of Lieutenant Theodore Laidley

by

James M. McCaffrey

J. M. McCaffrey

V. 6 War and the Southwest Series

University of North Texas Press
Denton, Texas

5   4   3   2   1

The paper in this book meets the minimum requirements of the
American National Standard for Permanence of Paper for Printed Library
Materials, Z39.48-1984

Permissions
University of North Texas Press
PO Box 311336
Denton TX 76203-1336

Library of Congress Cataloging-in-Publication Data

Laidley, Theodore, 1822–1886.
     Surrounded by dangers of all kinds : the Mexican War letters of Lieutenant
Theodore Laidley / edited by James McCaffrey.
          p.   cm.
     Includes bibliographical references (p.   ) and index.
     ISBN 1-57441-034-2 (cloth : alk. paper)
     1. Laidley, Theodore, 1822–1886—Correspondence. 2. Mexican War, 1846–
1848—Personal narratives, American. 3. Soldiers—West Virginia—Cabell
County—Correspondence. 4. Cabell County (W. Va.)—Biography. I. McCaffrey,
James M., 1946–   . II. Title.
     E411.L34   1997
     973.6'2'092—dc21   97-22086
     [b]   CIP

Design by Accent Design and Communications
Cover artwork, James T. Shannon, "Siege of Puebla, Began Sept. 13th. ended
Oct. 12th. 1847. 1850." Chromolithograph. 1987.91. © Amon Carter Museum,
Fort Worth, Texas

Contents

Acknowledgments

The Mexican War letters of Lieutenant Theodore Laidley came to my attention while researching my earlier *Army of Manifest Destiny*.[1] These letters, which reside in the DeGolyer Library at Southern Methodist University in Dallas, Texas, struck me as being very noteworthy in that they were written by an officer who, although he missed the amphibious landing at Veracruz, did take part in the later siege of Puebla.

Lieutenant Laidley wrote these letters in a clear hand, and they are easy to read. His spelling and grammar are generally good, and I have left them as I found them. Since paper was often at a premium, Laidley and many other letter writers of the time apparently made maximum use of what they had by not always breaking their prose into discernible paragraphs. In the interest of making the letters easier to read I have added paragraph breaks where they seemed appropriate. For the most part, however, the letters that follow are just as the young army officer wrote them a century and a half ago.

A number of people and organizations have contributed to this project. I would like to thank several people for their help. Curator Kay Bost at the DeGolyer Library made these letters available to me, and this book obviously could not have been published without her cooperation. Archivist Dru Bronson-Geoffroy at the Springfield Armory National Historic Site in Springfield, Massachusetts, supplied the photograph of Colonel Laidley. Assistant Archivist Judith A. Sibley at the United States Military Academy graciously provided a wealth of information on Laidley's days as a cadet there, and Museum Specialist Walter J. Nock of the West Point Museum supplied very detailed information on the captured cannons which Laidley sent back to his alma mater from the battlefields of Mexico.

The archives staff at the Library of Virginia sent information on the presentation of swords to volunteer officers from that state. I am also, quite obviously, indebted to the authors of all the various works cited in the notes.

---

[1] James M. McCaffrey, *Army of Manifest Destiny: The American Soldier in the Mexican War, 1846–1848.* New York: New York University Press, 1992.

Early Life of T. T. S. Laidley

Lieutenant Theodore Thadeus Sobieski Laidley was a young army officer during the Mexican War, and like so many of his fellow soldiers he wrote long letters home describing all the new and unusual sights he saw and events he experienced. He told of landing at Veracruz,[1] on the Mexican coast in March 1847, and assisting in the reduction of that important port city. He gallantly commanded a field battery at Cerro Gordo the following month as Major General Winfield Scott began his march into the interior of Mexico, with the capital city as his ultimate goal. The young lieutenant did not accompany Scott all the way into the valley of Mexico, but remained with the garrison at Puebla, where his actions were instrumental in denying that city to Santa Anna in a month-long siege in the fall of 1847.

John Osborne Laidley and Mary Scales Hite Laidley were among the earliest settlers of Cabell County along the Ohio River in far western Virginia. It was there, in the village of Guyandotte, that Theodore Laidley was born on April 14, 1822. He was the third of twelve children and the first son.

Theodore's ultimate decision to seek a military career was merely in keeping with family custom, and might even have been expected. His grandfather, Thomas Laidlaw, had emigrated to North America from Scotland as a young man of eighteen in 1774. This put him here on the very eve of the American Revolution, and although some members of his family remained loyal to King George III he cast his lot with the colonists and enlisted in George Washington's army. He changed his surname to Laidley, so the story goes, so as not to be confused with the Loyalist branch of his family. Theodore's father, John, continued the military tradition, or perhaps it was just an anti-British tradition, by serving for a time with a company of Virginia volunteer artillery during the War of 1812.[2]

Shortly after his fifteenth birthday, Theodore Laidley entered Ohio University at Athens. He was a good student in all of the basics of reading, writing, mathematics, and geography, and it did not take him long to master French which he soon was reading with relative ease. His course of study also had him poring over several works in classical Latin. By early 1838, however, he apparently had decided on a military career and sought to obtain an appointment to the United States Military Academy at West Point if at all possible.[3]

Laidley's professors at Ohio University certified his academic progress and attested to his high moral character while Ohio Congressman Calvary Morris recommended him to the secretary of war for consideration as a cadet. On February 12, 1838, Secretary of War Joel Poinsett offered Laidley an appointment at West Point contingent upon his passing the entrance exam. Young Theodore and his family must have discussed the offer at some length because he did not accept it for more than three weeks. Then, however, on March 7, he wrote in a clear bold hand: "I accept the appointment which the President of the United States has honored me with and will repair to West Point as directed."[4]

Having accepted the appointment and promised to serve for the legally specified time following his graduation, he left home and reported to West Point sometime between June 1 and June 20, 1838. There do not appear to be any extant letters from him during his cadet days, but his experiences at West Point were probably typical of others. Upon arrival at the academy, probably by river boat from New York City, Laidley would have climbed the hill from the wharf to the Plain, or campus. His first stop would have been at the adjutant's office where he would have signed in and turned over any cash he happened to have, since cadets were not allowed to have any money while at the academy. Once on the books he would have received a room assignment in the barracks where he would live until the up-coming entrance examinations.[5]

Educational prerequisites for incoming cadets were not very rigorous, even by contemporary standards, and they undoubtedly presented no difficulty for the young man from western Virginia. Incoming cadets had to be able to read and write and solve simple mathematical problems. As part of the process, each newcomer also had to undergo a physical examination, most of which was performed visually. The doctor measured his height, weighed him, checked him for obvious tooth decay, bunions, and any noticeable skeletal malformations that might inhibit full use of his limbs. There was also a vision check, but it was not particularly scientific. As one former cadet recalled years later, the doctor stood at the far side of the room with a dime in his hand "and we were required to tell whether it was heads or tails."[6]

There were 111 aspiring army officers entering the class of 1842, and as they arrived they began to form friendships that would last some of them forever. There were seven other Virginians destined to graduate with Laidley, and he doubtless gravitated toward them, at least at first, out of a sense of state solidarity.

Some of the newcomers were the sons of military figures. The father of Cadet Mansfield Lovell, for example, was Surgeon General Joseph Lovell, while Henry Eustis, Henry Whiting, Henry Stanton, Charles Baker, and James Abert all were sons of army officers, and Christopher Perry's father was renowned naval hero Oliver Hazard Perry. Many other incoming cadets managed to make names for themselves even without the benefit of militarily influential fathers. From Ohio came future Civil War army commander William S. Rosecrans, while several southern states produced cadets that would eventually wear Confederate gray. From Mississippi came Earl Van Dorn, while Lafayette McLaws arrived from Georgia, and South Carolina sent Daniel H. Hill and James Longstreet. In fact, twenty-two of the thirty-eight cadets who eventually graduated with Laidley and lived until 1861 were destined to wear the stars of general officers during the Civil War—thirteen in the Union Army and nine in the Confederate Army. Another of Laidley's classmates was present at Fort Sumter at the commencement of hostilities in 1861, but is probably more famous for something he did *not* do. New York's Abner Doubleday is widely, and erroneously, credited with inventing the game of baseball.[7]

July 1, 1838, marked graduation day at the Military Academy. Such later well-known soldiers as Pierre G. T. Beauregard and William J. Hardee received their commissions that day, and as they made their transitions from cadets to regular army officers, members of each of the lower classes were also promoted. The graduating first classmen, or seniors, received either regular or brevet commissions as second lieutenants, and each of the other classes moved up one slot. For Laidley and the other newly arrived men, their status now changed from virtual nonentities, or "Things," to plebes, or fourth class cadets. The graduates soon left the Academy for their assignments, the new second classmen left for their only furlough during their West Point years, and the rest of the corps of cadets went into summer camp nearby.

Beginning in summer camp and extending over the next four years, Laidley would find that his every waking moment would be regulated by the sounds of drums and fifes. They told him when to wake up, when to go to each of his meals, when to report for drill, and when to go to bed. It was also in summer camp that he and his classmates began to learn the intricacies of military drill—three times a day. They began in groups of four. This was the school of the soldier, where their instructors taught them the basics of how to stand at attention, how to execute the various facing movements properly, and, after receiving their flintlock muskets, how to perform the manual of arms.

Then, over the course of the summer, they learned the ever more intricate movements of companies and battalions. After a time, the plebes began receiving instruction in artillery drill as well, learning to fire the bronze six-pounder cannons of the time.

In a cadet's initial summer camp he and his classmates first became victims of the upperclassmen's practical jokes and hazing. Sometimes it was something as simple as seeing to the personal needs of the older students; making sure their muskets were cleaned and oiled, or keeping them well supplied with water. A favorite prank was to invite a naive plebe to receive his regulation haircut. Only the "barber's" imagination restricted the range of results. One man might find half of his hair neatly and expertly trimmed only to have the upperclassman wielding the scissors announce that he was finished. The next unsuspecting plebe might find that his hair cutter had snipped away with no apparent pattern, from which he emerged looking as if he suffered from a bad case of mange. Sometimes the older cadets would wait until the freshmen were settled into their tents for the night and then sneak in and steal their clothes, thereby requiring them to either fail to appear at the next morning's roll call or to take their places in the formation dutifully wrapped up in nothing more than a blanket. Offering more immediate comic gratification to the perpetrators than this would be to simply collapse the tents upon the newcomers after they had turned in.

Most of the hazing stopped when regular classes began in the fall, but there was still an occasional instance of it. Once, when an upperclassman was temporarily standing in for an absent professor, he ordered a plebe to "make a topographical sketch of your father's farm on a scale of one-ten-millionth, with a plan of all the buildings, and giving the tilled and unbroken land a fair evaluation as well as the buildings, stock, etc., including also all the money at interest, at the same time discounting for all outstanding debts. . . . To make your sketch more complete, I wish you to draw also a vertical projection of your grandfather as he appeared on receiving the intelligence of the Battle of New Orleans."[8]

Finally, near the end of August 1838, the second classmen returned from their furloughs, and Laidley and all of his new classmates packed up their tents and returned to the barracks for the beginning of their first academic year at the Academy. Typically, two cadets shared a room about thirteen feet square. It had two mattresses on the floor, two small tables, two small wooden chairs, a wooden water bucket with tin dipper, a small shaving mirror, and a crockery wash bowl. No curtains were permitted on the windows, and illumination for night time study was furnished by two small fish oil lamps, "the smell of which," recalled one former student, "was similar to, if not worse than, that which Jonah must have experienced during his sojourn in the whale's belly."[9]

The officers on duty at the Military Academy rigorously enforced discipline on their charges. Cadets might earn conduct demerits for such offenses as having liquor or playing cards in their possession, being out of their rooms after taps at night, or using profane language. In one case of rather extreme nitpicking, a cadet picked up some demerits for sitting in his room with his feet up on his desk. The crime—"defacing public property." Different transgressions carried different penalties, but if a cadet's total number of demerits reached 200 in any given year he faced expulsion. At the end of each spring term, Academy administrators posted the students' conduct rankings along with their academic ranks.[10]

Regulations required all cadets to attend Sunday church services en masse. They occupied the center section of the chapel where they sat on backless benches in their snug-fitting uniforms and tried not to earn any demerits by falling asleep during the sermons. This forced attendance at chapel met with some resentment. One cadet thought that such a practice was superfluous. Since the rest of their daily lives were so tightly regulated, they had hardly any time to do anything for which they should atone on Sunday. "It is almost as difficult to sin here," he commented, "as it is to do well in the world at large." Some, however, used their Sunday excursions to the chapel to sneak a forbidden chew of tobacco. In fact, at one point during Laidley's time there, the Commandant of Cadets had to plead with the cadets formally to discontinue this practice because it left the floor of the chapel so slippery with tobacco juice that the facility was unusable for evening services.[11]

A brand new three-story building provided all of the classrooms at the Academy. Class size was held to about twelve to fifteen students so the instructors could devote considerable attention to each of them. This class size also meant that every pupil would be called upon in every class every day. The cadets dared not be unprepared.

All of the students, regardless of their choice of military specialty after graduation, received the same academic preparation at the academy. In addition to their formal classroom training, all cadets practiced military drill every afternoon from 4 P.M. until sunset.

The French armies of Napoleon were still regarded as being well worthy of emulation, so all first-year students studied French six days per week. American military leaders believed that professional army officers should be able to read and translate works on military topics coming from France. The only other formal classroom course for freshmen was mathematics, and they spent the entire fall semester studying algebra.

Formal examinations took place in January for all students. Any man who failed even one course was recommended to the

Secretary of War for dismissal from the Academy. Plebes who successfully navigated these tests then went on to more French lessons and to study plane and solid geometry, plane and spherical trigonometry, and analytical geometry during the spring term. By the summer of 1839, Laidley's academic class rank was eighteenth out of a class that had been reduced by attrition to eighty-five during the first year. His thirty-nine demerits were well under the 200 allowable and placed him at number ninety-three out of the entire corps of cadets.[12]

Second-year students continued to study French, but their math course grew progressively more difficult. They now plodded through differential and integral calculus as well as land surveying. These third classmen also began learning topographical drafting and how to draw the human figure, and they took their first courses in the interestingly named Department of Ethics. In this phase of their education, presided over by the post chaplain, the students spent the first three months of the year studying English grammar and composition, followed by three and a half months of rhetoric and six weeks of geography.[13]

Laidley made a decision during his second year at the academy that would have a lifelong effect on him. One Sunday while all the cadets were in mandatory attendance at chapel, he stood up and declared himself desirous of being baptized. This was an important step for a seventeen year old to take, but, according to contemporaries, he never wavered in his religious devotion. In fact, his letters home from Mexico a few years later contain repeated references to his longing to attend church services again.[14]

After successfully completing the June examinations in 1840, Laidley stood at number eleven out of a class that was now down to seventy-six. He had also improved his conduct, earning only nineteen demerits and elevating his standing on the overall conduct roll to number seventy. He and his classmates then departed on their one and only extended furlough. There would be no summer camp for them that year.[15]

When Laidley and the others returned for their third year at West Point they were about to embark on the most intensive part of their schooling. They continued their drawing classes, and their chemistry classes now included inorganic, organic, and applied chemistry, as well as the study of gravity, electricity, and heat and light. Their fall semester mechanics class had them studying such technical subjects as the equilibrium of forces, strengths of materials, theory of pumps, fluid mechanics, electromagnetism, and the application of mechanics to the construction of machines. This was followed in the spring term by eight lessons on acoustics and optics, and then the rest of the semester was spent on the study of astronomy.

There were only sixty men left in Laidley's class by the end of their third year. He had continued his steady academic improvement, and when school officials posted the standings that year he had risen to number six. His thirteen demerits during the year had pushed his conduct rank up to number thirty-eight.[16]

At the summer camp following this third year of schooling, the new first classmen began learning the mysteries of ordnance. They saw how to manufacture gunpowder. They learned the use of rockets. They learned how to make the powder bags that were used in the cannons. It may well have been this hands-on exposure to the ordnance branch that caused Cadet Laidley to select that as his post-graduation specialty.

Upon returning to the classroom for their final year of study, the new seniors studied international and constitutional law, Supreme Court decisions, moral philosophy, and the laws of war in the Department of Ethics. For the first time they took courses in Professor Dennis Hart Mahan's Department of Civil and Military Engineering and the Art of War. This included a heavy emphasis on construction materials, wood framing, masonry, road building, railroads, canals, river and harbor improvements, and stonecutting as well as a considerable amount of engineering drawing practice. In the spring term they took classes in mineralogy and geology where they learned about the formation of coal, sandstone, and limestone. They saw how mountains and valleys evolved over time and how earthquakes and volcanoes occurred. They took a course in military engineering, or how to build permanent as well as field fortifications. This course also exposed them to a grand total of six lessons on the science of war. The graduates would leave West Point with a very solid base of technical knowledge, but with little real information on how to fight the kind of enemy most expected to encounter—Indians.[17]

Cadet First Classman Theodore Laidley and those others fortunate enough to have survived the rigors of the previous four years graduated on July 1, 1842. Shortly before graduation each of them had specified the branch of service he preferred, but class standing had a lot to do with whether or not they got what they wanted. The hierarchy of branch was: engineers, topographical engineers, ordnance, artillery, infantry, and dragoons or mounted rifles. "This scale," recalled an 1848 graduate, "was supposed to represent the brain requirement for each branch. We were taught with every breath we drew at West Point the utmost reverence for this scale; . . . the engineers were a species of gods, next to which came the 'topogs'—they were but demigods. Then came the ordnance, a . . . connecting link between the deities and ordinary mortals . . . the dragoons last. For the latter, a good, square seat in the saddle was deemed of more importance than brains." Graduation day in 1842 saw all but one of the top eight graduates choose the engineers. The exception was Laidley, who graduated number six and chose ordnance. Only one other man, James G. Benton, chose this branch of service, while two men went into the topographical engineers, eleven into artillery, twenty-three into the infantry, and six into the dragoons.[18]

The ordnance department had experienced a rather checkered existence up until this point. It had been disbanded altogether as part of the general demobilization following the Revolutionary War. Congress revived it on the eve of the War of 1812, but in 1821 it was merged with the artillery. It once again emerged as an independent department in 1832.

It was up to the ordnance department to supervise the manufacture and storage of small arms, artillery, and ammunition at the government arsenals. The chief of the department was also responsible for issuing contracts to private manufacturers when the need arose for them to supplement government production. This meant that ordnance officers had to have a certain amount of expertise in metallurgy and manufacturing techniques as well as the intended end use of the product. They must, for example, understand the needs of a field artillerist if they were to provide him with suitable weapons, and they must be prepared to function as artillerists themselves if the need should arise.[19]

Following graduation, brand new Lieutenants Laidley and Benton both received orders to report as assistant ordnance officers to Watervliet Arsenal just outside of Troy, New York, near the state capital at Albany. Already on duty at Watervliet when the two new officers reported was Josiah Gorgas from the class of 1841, destined to become the Confederacy's chief of ordnance. After a couple of years, Laidley transferred to Washington Arsenal and then returned once again to Watervliet in 1845. By that time, however, both Benton and Gorgas had gone on to other assignments.

The United States was fast approaching war with Mexico—our first foreign war—when Laidley began his second tour of duty at Watervliet. Trouble had been brewing between the neighboring republics for a number of years, trouble centering on a third North American republic—Texas.

Texas, ultimately the twenty-eighth state in the Union, was historically part of the Spanish colony of New Spain, but it was never heavily populated except by roving bands of Comanches and other native tribes. Mexico's leaders thought that an infusion of settlers from the United States might provide a spark to colonization by Mexican citizens. Secondarily, if the hoped for influx of Mexican colonists failed to materialize, at least the Americans would provide a buffer between the Comanches and the more settled areas of Mexico farther south.

The trickle of new Texans that began in the early 1820s soon reached flood proportions. By 1830, the Mexican government began to realize that perhaps it had made a mistake when opening Texas to foreigners. The 16,000 Anglo settlers greatly outnumbered the Mexicans. Not only were the newcomers more numerous than the natives, but there was an undercurrent of ethnic animosity in the Anglo settlements that only threatened to become more serious as the percentage of North Americans in Texas increased.

The Mexican congress responded by passing legislation on April 6, 1830, that sent more troops into Texas and stated that "the citizens of foreign countries lying adjacent to the Mexican territory are prohibited from settling as colonists in the states or territories of the republic adjoining such countries."[20] In other words, there was to be no more immigration from the United States into Texas.

This did not have the desired effect. If anything, it only made the Texians—as they were called—cling even more tenaciously to the rights they had enjoyed under the *U.S.* Constitution, and these did not include living in a garrison state. Even though further immigration from the United States was now illegal, Mexican authorities did not have the manpower to effectively seal their border.

By the fall of 1835, some Anglo-Texans openly advocated a complete break with the central government. A small skirmish near the town of Gonzales on October 2, led to open warfare between the colonists and the forces of Mexico. The small Mexican garrison at Goliad surrendered a week later, and on December 9, the Texians forced the surrender of a much larger force at San Antonio. Incensed, Mexico's leader, Antonio López de Santa Anna, vowed to teach the Americans a lesson and soon started northward at the head of an army determined to reinstate government rule.

By February 24, 1836, Santa Anna's army had reached the outskirts of San Antonio where, contrary to sound military judgment, about 150 Texians had barricaded themselves within the compound of the old abandoned mission known as the Alamo. A second Mexican army, under General José Francisco Urrea, was moving up the coast toward the much larger Anglo garrison at Goliad. Following a siege of almost two weeks, Santa Anna's men finally wiped out the Alamo defenders on March 6. Two weeks later Urrea's men defeated and captured the Goliad garrison. Then, on Palm Sunday, March 27, 1836, the captives—numbering almost four hundred—were marched out of their enclosure and summarily executed.

In the meantime, Texas statesmen declared their independence from Mexico on March 2, and named Sam Houston to head the fledgling Texas Army. After the two tragedies at the Alamo and at Goliad, Houston's men itched for revenge. On April 21, on the banks of the San Jacinto River, they got it. Shouting, "Remember the Alamo! Remember Goliad!" the Texians killed or captured virtually all of Santa Anna's army. The dictator himself escaped, but was captured the next day and forced to sign a treaty recognizing the independence of Texas from Mexico.

Even though Santa Anna repudiated the treaty as soon as he was again safe in Mexico, the deed had been done. Due to continued political turmoil in Mexico, Texas independence remained virtually unchallenged for quite some time. Most Texians favored immediate annexation to the United States, but when this was not forthcoming they chose independence over continued domination by Mexico.

When annexation failed to materialize—there was concern within the U.S. Senate over the prospect of adding to the power of the slave-holding South—Texas settled down to a period of time as an independent republic. Texas represented a vast domain, and Texas leaders increased it even more so by claiming a southern border of the Rio Grande River, thereby annexing by proclamation the northernmost part of the Mexican state of Tamaulipas, whose traditional border was at the Nueces River. By the summer of 1841, the United States, France, and Great Britain all had extended diplomatic recognition to the young republic.

James K. Polk's 1844 presidential campaign was based, in part, on a desire to add Texas to the Union. But when repeated attempts to get the Senate to ratify a treaty of annexation failed, he presented the issue to the full Congress in the form of a joint resolution. Unlike a treaty ratification, which required the affirmation of two-thirds of the Senators present to carry it into effect, the joint resolution merely required simple majorities in each house. As such, Texas annexation was approved in March, 1845, and sent to the people of Texas for a referendum.

While all of this had been going on, the Mexican government considered the steps being taken to separate Texas permanently from Mexico to be nothing less than an effort to steal part of the Mexican republic. As such, it was an act of war, and Mexico's ambassador to the United States, Juan N. Almonte, demanded his passport so he could return home. President Polk obviously did not view the annexation of Texas in the same light. He not only regarded Texas as having been a politically independent republic, but he also saw fit to honor its claim of all the land north of the Rio Grande River. This was a second slap in the face to Mexico. Not only was the United States attempting to steal the Mexican province of Texas, but part of the state of Tamaulipas as well.

Nevertheless, on June 29, 1845, Brevet Brigadier General Zachary Taylor received orders at Fort Jesup, Louisiana, to make his force ready to move into Texas while annexation was being finalized to protect that about-to-be-state from any possible Mexican attempts to reconquer it. He was to select a point on or near the Rio Grande that would be both healthful to his troops and well sited to stop a Mexican incursion. "You will limit yourself," his orders continued, "to the defence of the territory of Texas, unless Mexico should declare war against the United States." He was to do nothing to bring on a war. If, after arriving on the Rio Grande, he encountered Mexican outposts on the east bank, he was to leave them unmolested.[21]

It took a while for Taylor's small force to make the necessary arrangements for what would be a major change of station, but by July 25, the first elements began reaching the Texas coast near Corpus Christi, where the Nueces River flows into the Gulf of Mexico. Nor were Mexican forces idle. The nearest Mexican garrison to Corpus Christi was at Matamoros, 125 miles away on the Rio Grande, but reinforcements were rumored to be on the way.

[1] Veracruz is the modern spelling. Laidley used the spelling accepted in his day: Vera Cruz.

[2] John G. Butler, "Theodore T. S. Laidley," in *Seventeenth Annual Reunion of the Association of the Graduates of the United States Military Academy at West Point, New York* (East Saginaw, Michigan, 1886), 98; George Selden Wallace, "Laidley," in *Cabell County Annals and Families* (Richmond: Garrett and Massie, 1935), 425, 427, 428.

[3] Newton Peck to John Laidley, January 29, 1838, in National Archives Microfilm Publication 688, *U.S. Military Academy Cadet Application Papers, 1805–1866*.

[4] Andrew Beirne to Joel Poinsett, February 8, 1838 and Theodore Laidley to Joel Poinsett, March 7, 1838, both in National Archives Microfilm Publication 688, *U.S. Military Academy Cadet Application Papers, 1805–1866*.

[5] Theodore Laidley to Joel R. Poinsett, March 7, 1838, National Archives Microfilm Publication 688, *U.S. Military Academy Cadet Application Papers, 1805–1866*; John C. Tidball, "Getting Through West Point: The Cadet Memoirs of John C. Tidball, Class of 1848," ed. James L. Morrison, Jr. *Civil War History* 26, no. 4 (December 1980), 312.

[6] Tidball, 312.

[7] Judith A. Sibley, Assistant Archivist, United States Military Academy, to James McCaffrey, September 5, 1995; George W. Cullum, *Biographical Register of the Officers and Graduates of the U.S. Military Academy at West Point, New York Since its Establishment in 1802*, Supplementary Vol. VI-A, ed. Wirt Robinson (Saginaw, Michigan: Seeman and Peters, 1920), 44–46; Ezra J. Warner, *Generals in Gray: Lives of the Confederate Commanders* (Baton Rouge: Louisiana State University Press, 1959), 282.

[8] Tidball, 104–106; Stephen A. Ambrose, *Duty, Honor, Country: A History of West Point* (Baltimore: Johns Hopkins University Press, 1966), 158.

[9] James Lunsford Morrison, Jr., "The United States Military Academy, 1833–1866: Years of Progress and Turmoil" (Ph.D. diss., Columbia University, 1970), 113; Tidball, 307.

[10] Ambrose, 150.

[11] Ambrose, 151–52; Tidball, 311.

[12] *Register of the Officers and Cadets of the U.S. Military Academy*, (June 1839), 14, 22.

[13] Morrison, 148–71, 299–303; Tidball, 316–23.

[14] Butler, 100.

[15] *Register of the Officers and Cadets of the U.S. Military Academy*, (1840), 10, 12, 17.

[16] *Register of the Officers and Cadets of the U.S. Military Academy*, (1841), 11–12, 19.

[17] Morrison, 148–71, 299–303; Tidball, 316–23.

[18] Tidball, 323–24; Cullum, II, 109–52.

[19] Constance McLaughlin Green, Harry C. Thomson, and Peter C. Roots, *The Ordnance Department: Planning Munitions for War* (Washington, D.C.: Office of the Chief of Military History, Department of the Army, 1955), 14–16.

[20] Barker, 266.

[21] Serial Set 485, House Document 196, 29th Congress, 1st Session, 70.

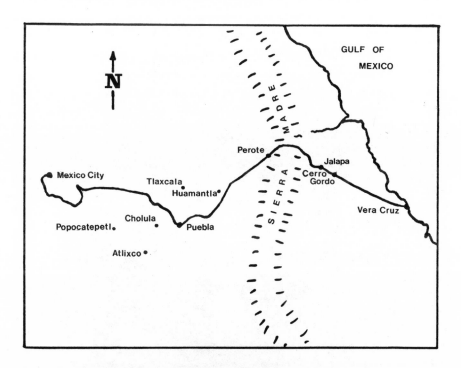

Approximate route of the American Army from Vera Cruz to Mexico City

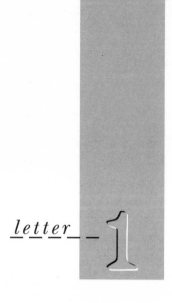

letter _ _ 1

Most of Lieutenant Laidley's first letter home sounds just like a letter from any young man away from his family. About the only concession he makes to the possibility of war is musing about the heat in that part of the world and making the universal point that whatever else a war may bring about it is a good place for career army officers to earn official notice and promotion. For that reason he is anxious to be assigned to Taylor's command if war comes.

Watervliet Arsenal N.Y.
August 23$\underline{rd}$ 1845

My dear father

Your favor has been received for a week, and truly gratifying to me was it to hear of Lou's convalescence and of her anticipated visit to Cabell. A lonesome life must it be that she leads in the wilds of Missouri, and an expedited recovery may justly be

1

expected from her being surrounded by her friends and many comforts that she would be deprived of in the west.

Since my last to you, we have been most busy in making and sending off stores for Texas—Orders for supplies succeeded each other in quick succession, all requiring the utmost despatch, and quite busy has it kept us in getting off the required stores.

Previously, the packing up of ammunition was connected with no sensation, no feeling other than would follow the packing up of so much mud or anything else, but when we have taken so much care in the perfect adjustment of the cartridges and balls and preparing everything for <u>actual use</u> the feeling of indifference is changed, and we cannot view them, each one, perhaps, in a short time, to be the avenged messenger of death to some poor Mexican, the same as if they were to be put away in store to be used you know not when, where or against whom, if ever.

You have doubtless, seen account of the troops sent to Texas. They have sent four regiments and parts of others, embracing Infantry Artillery and Cavalry. More companies of flying artillery which would deal out death and destruction to the Mexicans if they could ever get them within the range of grape or canister shot.

In addition, they have ordered two officers from each corps to join Genl Taylor, who has the command. This will give him a large Staff and will render the duty very pleasant to all on it.

There is a great objection, and the only one, to going down at this season of the year, the great danger of not being able to stand the climate which will be particularly trying to all who leave the north at this time to go there in the midst of the most unhealthy Season.

Otherwise, it would be pleasant and desirable duty, giving one an opportunity of seeing service that an officer in our service rarely sees, at the same time giving him a fair opportunity of distinguishing himself and of advancement in his profession.

Mexico has been acting the part of b[r]aggadocio and making the most extravagant threats, but whether she declares war against the States is extremely problematical, and many are of the opinion that she will not.

The latest intelligence rather goes to favor the opinion that she will attack the Texicans in hope of conquering them again and thus bring on a war without declaring war against us, but endeavor to throw the odium of beginning the war upon the States.

Not much is expected however from troops half fed, half clothed, half paid as her's are, but the worst would be from the Indians that she would not fail to set against us, and harass the border inhabitants, and the innumerable privateers that would be fitted out by vagabonds of all nations sailing under her flag to molest our commerce. In that way it might and most probably would be a troublesome affair for the United States and but little glory to be won by fighting with such an enemy.

There is a good deal of feeling among the officers and a desire to be sent down there to the field of action.

We have been suffering very much from the heat and drought, to see what warm weath[er] they have here one would be led to suppose that they could never have very cold, but there are the greatest extremes and the variations sometimes are most rapid.

I have been anxious to go to the seashore for a week but have been so busy that I have not been able to get off, and now we regard the summer as being nearly over and the inhabitants of the city beginning to return.

I may however get down to New York to see the Great Britain, the monster in the way of Ships, iron Ships. She is regarded as well worth visiting and will pay one for his trouble.

It is astonishing how they annihilate time and space. We hear from our traveling friends abroad in fourteen days after they write, almost as soon as from many parts of the United States and sooner than many others.

I have not heard anything about the disposition of officers for this winter, and it is not likely that we will for a couple of months. We have news of one having been ordered to this post from Fort Monroe, Old Point Comfort whose place was filled by one sent from St. Louis. But what will be my home for the winter I am very patiently waiting to hear making up my mind to be content with whatever they give me.

I hope I shall have no difficulty in doing it. [T]hat it will not require me to call in play my powers of patience.

I have been trying to go to Montreal and Quebec but have not succeeded through want of a travelling companion and owing to our late press of business.

Give my love to all.

I remain your affectionate son.

Theodore

Even though General Taylor's force had already arrived in Texas when Lieutenant Laidley wrote this letter, war with Mexico was not yet imminent, and he seems convinced that the troubles between the two countries may be resolved without taking that final step. As a professional soldier, of course, he was not unaware that he soon might be required to go to war, but that possibility was still remote enough to allow him to write of other, more mundane, matters.

His married sister Louise has apparently been suffering from some unspecified illness, and he expresses brotherly concern about her continued recovery. His proposed travel plans include a trip to New York City to view the ultramodern, iron-hulled British steamer *Great Britain*. Truly a sight to behold, the big ship had arrived in New York only two weeks earlier with sixty passengers and 800 tons of cargo on its maiden transatlantic voyage. It carried 1,700 square yards of sail on its six masts to augment its 1,000-horsepower engine. Designed to carry 360 passengers if necessary, the *Great Britain* was the first screw-propelled steamer in regular transatlantic service.[1]

---

[1] W. A. Baker and Tre Tryckare, *The Engine Powered Vessel: From Paddle-Wheeler to Nuclear Ship* (New York: Grosset and Dunlap, 1965), 43, 45–46, 53.

At an October 16, 1845, cabinet meeting, President Polk, after having received assurances that Mexico was willing to negotiate a peaceable solution to the two countries' problems, decided to attempt to reopen relations. He selected Louisiana's John Slidell to perform this delicate diplomatic duty. Slidell was to attempt to convince the Mexican government that it was pointless to contest the annexation of Texas, and that the United States would insist upon the Rio Grande as that new state's border. He was also to offer to buy New Mexico—at that time encompassing parts of the present day states of New Mexico, Arizona, and Nevada—and Upper California. The president guessed that a reasonable price range for these vast holdings would be in the neighborhood of fifteen to twenty million dollars, but he wanted them badly enough that he was prepared to offer as much as forty million.

Difficulty over Slidell's mission arose almost immediately. Mexican Foreign Minister Manuel de la Peña y Peña had agreed to receive an American commissioner empowered to deal with the "present dispute"—which was the presence of American warships off the coast of Veracruz and the ongoing disagreement as to the status of Texas. Slidell, however, departed for Mexico clothed in the powers and with the title of minister plenipotentiary. He thereby had authority from Washington to negotiate any and all areas of interest between the two governments. Peña was not pleased when the American diplomat reached Mexico City on December 8, 1845. He had agreed to accept an agent of much lesser status. To have accepted Slidell would mean a de facto reopening of full diplomatic intercourse with the United States—a step that Mexico was as yet unwilling to take.

Nor were relations with the United States the only thing to cause anxiety for Mexico's President José Joaquín de Herrera. Internal politics continued to be very volatile. General Mariano Paredes y Arrillaga, a political rival of Herrera's, used the arrival of Slidell, and his presumed *acceptance* by the president, as a rallying cry to overthrow the government. He did so on January 2, 1846, and had himself named acting president. He then assured his constituents that he had no intention of giving in to North American desires for more Mexican territory and that he meant to regain Texas.

In light of the deteriorating international situation, President Polk, on January 13, instructed Secretary of War William L. Marcy to order General Taylor's small army to move from the Nueces to the Rio Grande. Taylor's orders, which he received on February 3, certainly did not consist of a blank check authorizing him to seek an encounter with Mexican troops. "It is not designed," they read, "in our present relations with Mexico, that you should treat her as an enemy; but, should she assume that character by a declaration of war, or any open act of hostility towards us, you will not act merely on the defensive if your relative means enable you to do otherwise."[1]

While the American troops began preparing for the move, a peaceful solution seemed to be slipping away, but all was not gloomy in Washington. Secretary of State James Buchanan, apparently finally aware of the diplomatic insult conveyed by Slidell's title, revised the wording of his appointment to that of a simple commissioner and sent it on to him to present to the authorities of the new Mexican government. Perhaps in this way the opposing diplomats might settle at least the Texas question without having to resort to war. Later, perhaps, another attempt could be made to acquire New Mexico and California peacefully.

The soldiers at Corpus Christi received word of their new destination with eager anticipation. Many still did not believe that Mexico would actually risk a war with them over Texas, but they had grown bored with camp life and looked forward to new surroundings. Taylor's dragoons and artillerymen broke camp on the morning of March 8, 1846, and over the next four days they and their infantry cousins slowly took up the march toward the Rio Grande. They faced no opposition for several days, although advance scouting parties occasionally encountered small bands of curious Mexicans. As the Americans approached the Colorado River on March 19, however, their levels of anticipation rose perceptibly. Mexican Captain José Barragan let General Taylor know that if he attempted to cross that river there would be bloodshed. Undeterred, Taylor deployed his artillery to cover the crossing. The soldiers cautiously waded into the sluggish stream the next morning, ever alert to the first signs of Mexican resistance. As they scrambled up the opposite bank they saw a few Mexican horsemen riding away in the distance. Perhaps Captain Barragan's ploy had only been a bluff.

On March 24, General Taylor began setting up a supply depot at Point Isabel, about ten miles up the coast from where the Rio Grande empties into the Gulf of Mexico. Supplies and, if need be, reinforcements could land there easily from ocean-going ships. The bulk of the army proceeded toward the Mexi-

can village of Matamoros, and on March 28, the advance elements arrived at the Rio Grande opposite the Mexican town.
General Taylor, in the spirit of his orders of January 13, immediately sent a messenger to his opposite number, Brigadier General Francisco Mejía, to assure him that the Americans meant
no harm to the citizens of Matamoros. They were only there to
ensure the safety of the new border of the United States.
Whether Mejía was reassured by this message or not, he was
militarily too weak to oppose his visitors without reinforcements,
and while both military commanders awaited political developments they set their troops to erecting protective earthworks
against the possible need for them. The American soldiers
named their earthen-walled compound "Fort Texas" in honor
of the country's newest state.

On April 12, Major General Pedro de Ampudia, the newly
arrived interim commander of Matamoros, gave Taylor twenty-
four hours to begin removing his entire command back to Corpus Christi or some other point north of the Nueces while the
two governments tried to resolve their differences. Taylor immediately replied that he was but a poor soldier and therefore
unqualified to discuss international politics. And since he, like
Ampudia, *was* a soldier, the Mexican commander surely should
understand that his orders would not permit him to retreat.
Before Ampudia could put into execution his preparations to
enforce his demand he learned Major General Mariano Arista
was on his way north to replace him.

Arista reached Matamoros on April 24, 1846. The Mexican
garrison there now consisted of approximately 5,000 men, and
the new commander would not wait long to put them to use.
The very next day he sent a 1,600-man force across the river to
try to cut Taylor off from his base of supplies at Point Isabel.
When word of the crossing reached Taylor he sent out a couple
of squadrons of dragoons to reconnoiter and either verify or

refute the information. The same day it blundered into a Mexican ambush and almost the entire eighty-man patrol was killed, wounded, or captured. Among the fatalities was George Mason, a fellow Virginian and West Point classmate of Theodore Laidley's. In Taylor's report of the clash to Washington he wrote that "hostilities may now be considered as commenced."[2]

This first engagement of the war was not an isolated event, but was the forerunner of an ambitious Mexican plan to isolate Taylor's main body from Point Isabel. To that end General Arista began crossing the bulk of his army over the Rio Grande about a dozen miles downriver from Matamoros on April 30. The next day Taylor, leaving a small force to protect his works along the river, led the rest of his command toward Point Isabel to both protect that vital link and to bring supplies back to Fort Texas.

General Taylor recognized the gravity of his situation and called on the governor of Louisiana to raise and forward to him immediately four regiments of infantry volunteers. This reinforcement, along with his regulars and some mounted Texas Rangers, would probably be enough for his immediate needs, but not everyone within the army looked forward to the arrival of more volunteers. Lieutenant George G. Meade, for example, hoped that a major battle might take place soon, before the arrival of additional troops. "We are anxious," he wrote his wife, "to give them [the Mexicans] a sound thrashing before the volunteers arrive, for the reputation of the army; for should we be unable to meet them before they come, and then gain a victory, it would be said the volunteers had done it, and without them we were useless. For our own existence, therefore, we desire to encounter them." Meade was soon to get his wish.[3]

Taylor reached Point Isabel before Arista could intercept him so some of the Mexican force turned back to lay siege to the five hundred Americans defending Fort Texas. By the afternoon of May 7, Taylor felt that he had strengthened his supply point sufficiently to resist any likely Mexican attack and started back to the Rio Grande with two hundred wagons loaded with supplies. When Arista learned of this movement he immediately began to consolidate his force to block Taylor's path. The two sides made tentative contact at about noon on May 8 near Palo Alto, and both commanders made final dispositions of their troops for battle.

The Battle of Palo Alto, the first major battle of the war, began about two o'clock and lasted until almost dark. By that time over a hundred Mexican soldiers lay dead, many of them the victims of superbly handled American artillery. The outnumbered Americans, on the other hand, had only lost five men killed.[4] Neither side had won a clear cut victory, and soldiers of both armies spent a nervous night waiting for the continuation of hostilities the next day.

The next morning, a Saturday, the Americans were surprised to see the Mexican army slowly making its way back toward the Rio Grande. General Taylor called a council of war with his senior subordinates to ponder what to do next and decided to follow along. About half way to the river, General Arista stopped his force in a dried up, former bend in the river called Resaca de la Palma. It was a naturally strong defensive position, so strong, in fact, that one Mexican general later said that he would have bet $10,000 that no army of 10,000—let alone Taylor's 2,000 or so—could have driven them from it. But in spite of the strength of the position, Taylor had little choice but to attack if he was going to reach Fort Texas. The battle began at mid-afternoon, and this time it was the American infantry that carried the brunt of the fighting. Losses were heavier on both sides before Mexican resistance collapsed. The retreat soon became a rout as the survivors began streaming toward the Rio Grande. Many drowned in their panic-stricken attempts to swim back across the river to safety at Matamoros.[5]

The battles of May 8 and 9, 1846, were not mere skirmishes. They marked irrevocable steps toward war.

Even while American and Mexican soldiers had been preparing to slug it out in the hot Texas sun at Resaca de la Palma, President Polk was polling his cabinet on the advisability of going to war with Mexico to settle the Texas question and to get possession of California. With the telegraph still in its infancy there was as yet no word in Washington of any armed clashes along the border. Nevertheless, most of the cabinet members now believed that the United States had explored all diplomatic avenues and found them ineffective. Only Secretary of the Navy George Bancroft voted against war, but he qualified his position by adding that his vote would of course change if American troops were attacked. Later that afternoon the president finally got the first word of the skirmish of April 25. He called his cabinet members back into an emergency meeting to apprise them of this latest bit of news, and this time there was no problem reaching a unanimous decision to ask congress for a declaration of war.

Polk spent Sunday preparing the war message that he would send Congress on Monday, informing it that in spite of the president's best efforts to reach peaceful accommodation, his "cup of forbearance had been exhausted. . . . Mexico has passed the boundary of the United States, has invaded our territory, and shed American blood upon the American soil."[6] Congress responded two days later, May 13, 1846, with a declaration of war that earmarked $10 million to prosecute the war and authorized the president to accept up to 50,000 volunteers.

Not all Americans were convinced that the war with Mexico was being pursued for reasons as noble as President Polk had listed in his message to Congress. Some, particularly in the north and northeast, saw the war as simply an excuse to obtain more land into which to extend slavery. Nevertheless, when the call went out for volunteers to serve in the army, the response was overwhelming. The War Department assigned each state governor a quota based upon population and asked him to raise that number of troops. So eager were young men to take part in what they probably believed would be their generation's best chance to achieve martial glory that they flooded into the hastily set up recruiting offices to offer their services. In every instance, the number of volunteers exceeded the government requirements. The governor of Illinois was asked to provide four regiments, about four thousand men, but Illinoisans stepped forward in numbers enough to fill fourteen regiments. The states of Ohio and Tennessee each had quotas of three thousand men. Ohioans filled up that number in two weeks, and in Tennessee enough men came forward to fill that state's ranks ten times over. The governor of Tennessee had to resort to drawing lots to see which volunteer companies would be allowed to serve and which would have to remain behind.[7]

Individual volunteers were usually not accepted into service, so prominent citizens—businessmen or politicians—took it upon themselves to raise enough recruits to fill a company. Then, when enough men had come forward, usually about a hundred, the company's organizer would offer his unit's services to the governor as part of that state's quota. After enough companies had been tendered and received they were formed into regiments and sent off to war, usually with just the barest essentials of military training.

There was disappointment in the ranks of those companies whose captains had not gotten them accepted for service, but many found other methods to reach the war. Some would-be soldiers crossed state boundaries and offered their services individually to recruiting agents there. In other cases, entire companies did the same thing. In this manner, Mississippians composed one entire company of Louisiana's regiment. When other Mississippians sought to do the same thing they found they were too late; Louisiana's quota was full. Undeterred, these men traveled at their own expense to Point Isabel, Texas, where they were mustered into service as part of the First Texas Infantry Regiment.[8]

The volunteers arrived at General Taylor's camp with varying degrees of preparation. There were, as yet, no such thing as basic training camps, even within the regular army. Some of these novice soldiers had seen prior service as volunteers against the Seminoles in Florida, a few were graduates of the U.S. Military Academy, but most were complete innocents when it came to the profession of arms. Many believed they could learn soldiering easily "on the job."

Whatever the inequities in preparation among them, one thing most of them did share was a sea voyage to get them to the theater of war. Most of the early volunteer units came from states within the Ohio or Mississippi valleys. Once formed into regiments they took passage downriver to New Orleans, from whence they sailed across the Gulf of Mexico to the camps near the mouth of the Rio Grande. Regiments from the eastern states reported later, and some of these men sailed from Atlantic ports such as New York, Boston, or Charleston, all the way to Brazos Santiago or, later, to Veracruz. But no matter the length of voyage, seasickness seemed to be a very common complaint. One volunteer described the voyage in less than glowing terms. He was one of about two hundred Indiana volunteers crammed aboard a small ship. Their sleeping quarters were below deck, and on a tossing sea this crowded, unventilated area quickly became unbearable. Even if a man managed to stay clear of seasickness himself, not all of those around him were likely to be so fortunate. "Sometimes you would find yourself eating," he wrote, "and someone close by would let slip right on your dinner and your clothes; and then you will imagine how pleasant our trip was." One South Carolinian, after an unforgettable three-day bout with seasickness, announced that his long held desire to go to sea had been completely satisfied.[9]

And when seasickness struck, the last thing most men wanted to do was eat, knowing that there was little likelihood they would be able to keep food down. A Mississippian crossing the Gulf in the summer of 1846 preferred to stay up on deck and "ate nothing from Wednesday morning until Sunday." A Virginia volunteer making the trip a year later tried a similar tactic but without much result. "For a week or more," he wrote, "I scarcely left the cabin, ate scarcely anything, and in fact did nothing but drink a little water or suck a piece of ice and throw up bile. The quantity of this latter that I discharged would astound a landsman." Even so, these men sometimes became the victims of practical jokers from among the men who remained unaffected by, or had recovered from, seasickness. One trick was to approach a suffering individual with news of a sure-fire cure. When the victim begged to be told what it was, the jokester would say, "Take first a good, thick slice of fat pork tied to a string." Usually that was all that needed to be said because the mere mention of the greasy meat would send the sufferer heading for the ship's rail again.[10]

For some men the seasickness lasted only a short time, and the rest of their voyage passed without complaint. Others seemed to be sick the entire time. They hung over the rail and, as an Indiana volunteer euphemistically put it, "cried 'New York' quite lustily." A Georgian painted a similar scene when he confided to his journal that "the decks were soon covered with the sick soldiers. [N]othing co[u]ld be heared—but the bursting of the waves & the grones of the sick." So distressing did an Ohio volunteer find his entire trip across the Gulf that he afterward referred to it as his time in purgatory, meaning he was between heaven—the United States—and hell—Mexico.[11]

When these ships encountered storms at sea, a not uncommon occurrence, the misery only increased. It was then, too, that any horses or mules being transported became terrified and often broke free of their restraints. The rolling and pitching of the decks only frightened them more, and soon they were sliding and crashing into the cabins or anything else in the way. Many of them were badly injured, the worst of whom had to be destroyed.

Reaction within the ranks of the regular army to this massive buildup was generally less than positive. The regulars, after all, had acquitted themselves quite well in the two battles so far and some saw no reason to augment their force with temporary soldiers. They saw the newcomers as part-time soldiers with no training, but with powerful political connections at home that would result in newspapers assigning all the military honors that might be won to these, their hometown boys, instead of the regulars.

And they were right. The American people held the regular peacetime army in rather low esteem, seeing it as a haven for those men who were unable to earn a living doing anything else and hence a useless waste of tax dollars. Indeed, when Ulysses S. Grant returned home in uniform after graduating from West Point in 1843, even a little boy in the street mocked his uniform and taunted him as being unfit for any honest labor.[12] With the coming of war, of course, this attitude changed a little. Then the army was valuable, it served a definite purpose and the general populace did not look down upon it quite so much. Communities across the country, although generally supportive of the war effort, still found it difficult to identify with the regular army. Since soldiers in the regular regiments came from all parts of the country there was no proprietary feeling in the various towns and villages toward the army. But it was different with the volunteers. They were local lads who went into service together. Hometown folk could follow news reports of battles and skirmishes and know whether or not their boys had been involved. Almost everyone in town knew someone in the local volunteer unit, and the newspapers fairly beamed with pride over their accomplishments. And since there were so very few independent news reporters traveling with the army, much of the hometown news came from the volunteers themselves, writing directly to the newspaper editors or writing to family members who then published their letters.

Lieutenant Daniel H. Hill, a classmate of Lieutenant Laidley's, probably expressed the feelings of the majority of regulars after the fighting at Palo Alto when he wrote that "it was a happy day . . . without a civilian in the ranks, to divide the victory of the 'regulars!'" He believed that had volunteer regiments taken part "they would have claimed the major part of the glory, and none can deny, that the American people would cheerfully have conceded it to them. Indeed, it would have been said, that the [regular] army was rescued from annihilation; and, unpopular as it was before, it would never again have held up its head." There would be plenty of time, after the arrival of thousands of volunteers, for this rivalry to grow more bitter.[13]

Meanwhile, back near the mouth of the Rio Grande, Mexican forces evacuated Matamoros about a week after their dual defeats at the hands of Taylor's army and fell back toward Monterrey, about 170 miles west. Taylor then spent the rest of the summer receiving reinforcements and accumulating the necessary supplies for continued operations against the enemy. His Texas Rangers scouted toward Monterrey to determine just how far in that direction the main body of enemy troops had gone and to ascertain whether this direct route would support the movement of Taylor's army in pursuit. The Texans were able to report that General Arista had indeed led the bulk of his command to Monterrey and that there was virtually no water along this road.

Taylor would have to find a different route to Monterrey. He decided to transport his men by river boat up the Rio Grande to the small Mexican village of Camargo near the mouth of the San Juan River. Here he would stockpile supplies and try to train the raw volunteers before attacking Monterrey. From Camargo he pushed a small force on to Cerralvo, about half way to Monterrey. Finally, on September 12, 1846, the American army began to move forward again.

A week later Taylor's command was drawn up just outside of its goal. The Mexican troops had had quite a long time to strengthen and fortify the city of 10,000, and its reduction would be no easy chore. Nevertheless, Taylor launched a two-pronged attack on September 20, and the next four days saw the most vicious fighting of the campaign yet. Fighting from house to house in the city, the combatants were sometimes so close as almost to be able to reach out their hands and touch one another. Finally, on September 24, the opposing commanders agreed to a truce. As a result of the ensuing negotiations the city surrendered to the Americans, but the defenders were allowed to evacuate to a point farther south for the duration of an eight-week armistice. Taylor and Arista both hoped that their governments would now be able to work out their difficulties and the war would not have to be resumed.

In the meantime, other American forces had also been busy. A combination of soldiers, sailors, marines, and American civilians managed to gain control of California with a minimum amount of bloodshed. Another hybrid force, made up of regular dragoons as well as mounted volunteers and infantry (including a battalion of 500 Mormon pioneers) pushed westward from Fort Leavenworth through parts of present-day Kansas and Colorado. On August 18, 1846, this Army of the West marched into Santa Fe, New Mexico. This vital trading center that had been so elusive to the Texan expedition of four years earlier fell to the Americans without a shot being fired.

The Mexican government made no serious effort to negotiate an end to the war following the Battle of Monterrey, so President Polk and his military advisers looked for a way to bring still more military pressure to bear. Perhaps if Mexico City itself were to come under attack it would serve notice to its leaders that their cause was hopeless. Such a move, however, would be a logistical nightmare. It was about six hundred miles from Monterrey to Mexico City, and much of it was over very forbidding terrain. For Taylor to make this march would mean not only subjecting his men to a very difficult trek through a hostile countryside, but it would also necessitate relying on a very long and exposed supply line back to the United States. A more logical plan might be to leave Taylor's force in place in northern Mexico, raise an additional army, and attack a port city, perhaps Tampico or Veracruz, and from there march inland to the Mexican capital.

There were reports that a good road ran from Tampico westward through San Luis Potosí and on toward the capital city, and that an American army could use this route to avoid a lot of the hostile terrain between Monterrey and Mexico City. Late in September, Secretary of War Marcy ordered General Taylor to detach Major General Robert Patterson with sufficient force to occupy Tampico. The U.S. Navy, under Commodore David Conner, was to have captured the city already so Patterson's force could arrive by ship and avoid a long march. Santa Anna was aware of the proposed move, but was unable to counter it. Instead he issued orders that the understrength garrison at

Tampico remove its heavy cannons to keep them from being captured, destroy whatever defenses they had built, and retreat upriver.

While the Mexican troops set about carrying out this order, Mrs. Anna Chase, the British wife of the expelled American consul at Tampico, wrote a letter to Commodore Conner alerting him to what was going on. A few days later the evacuation was complete, but it was still two and a half weeks before American ships appeared and formalized the capture of the town on November 14, 1846. Mrs. Chase made it apparent where her sympathies lay, in spite of her official status as a neutral, by flying a large American flag from the site of the former U.S. consulate to welcome the Americans. The first occupation troops arrived eight days after the navy and quickly discovered that the rumored road between there and San Luis Potosí was in fact just a rumor. This effectively eliminated Tampico from consideration as a jumping off point for an overland campaign against Mexico City. Veracruz might present a better option.

Major General Winfield Scott, the commanding general of the army, began preliminary planning for the capture of Veracruz soon after the fall of Monterrey. It would take time to put together the necessary force and to work out all the details of such a move, but there was little time to waste. It was imperative that any operation against Veracruz, or any other low-lying coastal target, be completed before the onset of the yellow fever season that regularly visited beginning in March or April. Although most local residents had become somewhat seasoned against the disease, it would be devastating to a foreign army.

Scott presented his plan to the president and other key advisors on October 17, 1846. He called for the use of 10,000 new troops and sufficient landing craft to get at least 2,500 of them ashore at one time. With these resources, Scott believed that the operation could begin by the first of the year and be completed well before the fever season began. But no plan is perfect and, among the problems with this one, two stood out. First, it would take some time to raise and train the requisite number of troops, which Scott later increased to 15,000. Second, the navy did not have *any* suitable landing craft.

Scott proposed to solve the manpower problem by having the secretary of war issue a call for the remainder of the originally authorized 50,000 volunteers—only about half had thus far been mustered into service—and by drawing a considerable percentage of the invasion force from Taylor's army. Taylor was not happy with this decision as it left him with virtually no dependable regular troops should Santa Anna venture north. There was probably also more than just a little bit of professional jealousy involved. General Taylor, after all, had made quite a name for himself by his conduct of the war so far. People were actively mentioning his name as a potential presidential candidate for the 1848 election. Perhaps General Scott, who was Taylor's commanding officer, wanted some of the glory for his own run for the White House.

Navy Lieutenant George M. Totten got to work on the second problem which was the fact that the U.S. Navy had no way to get the soldiers from the transport ships to the shore. Totten, however, soon designed a wide, flat-bottomed boat that fit the requirements of a landing craft. A naval officer would command the seven-man crew of each boat as it swept toward shore with forty combat equipped infantrymen aboard. Army contractors immediately set to work. They had one month to build 141 boats. Specifications called for them to be built in three sizes, ranging in length from 35 feet 9 inches to 40 feet so they could be nested together to conserve space on the transport ships carrying them to Mexico.[14]

Selection of an officer to be in command of this thrust into the heart of Mexico was frought with political considerations.

But there was another element in the equation. President Polk, a Democrat, recognized the likelihood that the war with Mexico might very likely produce the next American president, since Americans have often rewarded military heroes with election to the presidency. Both Taylor, who had already made a name for himself in the campaigns in northern Mexico, and Scott were Whigs. Missouri Senator Thomas Hart Benton, a Democrat and a close friend of the president, suggested that Polk appoint him to the rank of lieutenant-general so that he would outrank both Taylor and Scott. He could then oversee this second invasion of Mexico and claim for the Democrats all the resulting political credit. No such rank then existed in the U.S. Army, however, and its creation required the approval of congress. With congress not due to resume sessions for a while, the plan was reluctantly abandoned, and Polk grudgingly named Scott to personally lead the invasion force.

Scott left Washington on November 23. After stops in New York and New Orleans to arrange for supplies and shipping, he arrived at Brazos Santiago, near Point Isabel, on December 27, 1846.

This is the second letter in the collection, although Laidley surely must have written others in the intervening sixteen months. He had received orders to report for duty on General Scott's staff, an attractive enough position to cause many young officers to use whatever influence they had to get it. Usually this consisted of a letter of introduction and recommendation on their behalf to a commanding officer by some mutual acquaintance. Laidley, true to custom, carried such a communication to the commanding general even though he seems to have had at least a passing acquaintance with him already—perhaps they had been introduced to one another while Laidley was a cadet at West Point.

⁜ • ⁜

Head Quarters of the Army
Brazos San Iago, Jan 19th 1847

My dear Father

After a long, tedious and, to me, a disagreeable journey, I arrived here nearly a week since. We were delayed at Orleans a couple days, and then, at the mouth we stuck on the bar in crossing it where we remained four days longer before we could get off.

In the mean time a "Norther" came up and we had some experience in the sudden changes of the Southern climate. From a height of 86° the thermometer fell below zero and ice of considerable thickness was formed. We found great difficulty in keeping warm, with all the blankets, overcoats and cloaks that we could find.

We had a fresh wind and would have made quick passage but a strong current carried us some forty miles past our port before we made the land, this delayed our arrival to the 4th day from the mouth [of the Mississippi] and ninth from New Orleans.

I was not disappointed in my apprehensions as to seasickness, for I suffered very much—did not leave my birth or take anything to eat during the three days that we were out. I came to the firm determination never to go any journey by sea if it could possibly be avoided.

However it is now over and doubtless it will have a beneficial influence on my health—it is regarded as an excellent preparation for a campaign in this climate.

After waiting three or four hours a vessel came along side and asked for officers belonging to Gen. Scott's staff, took on board six of us and left the rest for another boat—much disgusted at the invidious distinction. It was very pleasant to get on firm land again without waiting all day but it proved the cause of having some of our baggage carried on to Tampico and there is no telling when if ever I get it again—almost everything I had except a few clothes. The Gen. professed to be very glad to see us. I gave him my letter from Mr. S. which he was glad to receive though he laughed at the idea of introducing me whom he had known so long. I am much of the opinion that it will be of service to me, in serving to render my duties more pleasant.

This is considerable of a port on the north end of an island of the same name, just opposite Pt. Isabel—a great depot for stores of all kinds. It is a sterile sandy low island, a few houses, great piles of stores, immense number of wagons and mules and a good deal of business in loading, unloading moving and moving stores, etc.

We are so fortunate as to have a small room large enough for four beds on the floor—where we sleep and stay. For our meals we go to the hotel which is a Mississippi steamboat run ashore where they give us steamboat fare for twenty dollars per month.

The Genl has a small mess but we have not rank enough to be of it. I have, however had the pleasure of dining with him and taking supper also, and can say that he lives very well though he seems to take pride in speaking of his pewter plates and cups.

We are doing nothing at present, occasionally he wants some writing done for him, but generally we have our time to ourself though not to leave for any length of time without special permission.

We expect to be hear till the 28th or 30th of this month when we will sail for Tampico. The troops are ordered to rendezvous about sixty miles below, and when they have all arrived, I presume we will make a strike on Vera Cruz.

I am somewhat afraid I shall be left behind at some depot where we land and not accompany the Genl further, however, there is no telling as the Genl is very fond of having a large staff. I shall not be detached if it be not absolutely necessary.

The weather is very changeable one day very pleasant, warm, the sun shining and real summer weather—in a few minutes, before you are aware of it the wind has shifted to the north and it is cold and disagreeable March weather. These northers last a day, two or three, and then it is delightful for so long when another comes on.

Everything sells at enormous prices and we are subjected to great expense while we remain here. At Tampico, I understand they fare better and pay less. We get fine fish here and turtles in great abundance. Venison is also plenty but of an inferior quality and poor beef. Water is the most difficult to obtain, being brought from the Mississippi or the Rio Grande and even that does not taste well.

Yesterday I rode up to the mouth of the Rio Grande 8 miles from this where are encamped over a thousand troops destined to form a part of the Genl's force.

I took a camp dinner and could not fail to form the contrast in my own mind between an officer of the Staff and line. I could never fancy the life of a line officer, they may be as jealous as they please and say what they choose—they are very envious and jealous of the staff, and they, with difficulty conceal their feelings.

My poor horse has suffered terribly and is now in no fit condition for a campaign. A number of the officers are apprehensive that they have lost theirs altogether—having been out 18 days and not heard from—so I ought to regard myself fortunate that I have got mine though half dead.

The rolling of the vessel in heavy seas bruised him and he was detained so long as to be almost starved.

I am anxious for a march, knowing that it would do me good, feeling so much better after my ride of sixteen miles yesterday. I shall write again about the time we leave here, and give you the news that there may be. Your letters will come safely if you direct to "Headquarters of the Army, Mexico."

My love to all.

Yours affectionately, Theodore.

Lieutenant Laidley has finally arrived in the war zone, although not without some trepidation. He probably had reached New Orleans by way of river boat down the Ohio and Mississippi Rivers, and the seasickness he suffered on his three-day journey across the Gulf of Mexico undoubtedly made him glad that he had not embarked from New York City and made the entire voyage by sea.

The young ordnance officer's perfunctory description of his sleeping quarters at least allows us to know that he was inside a building of some sort. Earlier arrivals, those who had come with General Taylor's original force, had not been that lucky. They had lived in leaky tents that let the rain, the heat of the sun, and swarms of insects in to disturb the slumber of those within.

---

[1] Serial Set 485 House Document No. 196, 29th Congress, 1st session, 77–78.

[2] Zachary Taylor to Adjutant General of the Army, April 26, 1846, House Executive Document, 29th Congress, 1st session, No. 196, 120; quoted in Ward McAfee and J. Cordell Robinson, *Origins of the Mexican War: A Documentary Source Book*, 2 vols. (Salisbury, N.C.: Documentary Publications, 1982), vol. 2, 149–50.

[3] George G. Meade to his wife, May 5, 1846; quoted in George Gordon Meade, *The Life and Letters of George Gordon Meade* (New York: Scribner's Sons, 1913), vol. 1, 76.

[4] The Mexican army entered the battle with 3,709 men and lost 102 killed, 129 wounded, and 26 missing. The American army began the day with 2,288 men and lost 5 killed, 48 wounded, and 2 missing. K. Jack Bauer, *The Mexican War* (New York: Macmillan, 1974), 57.

[5] The American losses were 33 killed and 89 wounded, while the Mexicans lost 154 killed, 205 wounded, and 156 missing. Bauer, 62–63.

[6] Serial Set 485, House Document 196, 29th Congress, 1st session, 5.

[7] Justin H. Smith, *The War with Mexico* (New York: Macmillan, 1919; reprint, Gloucester, Mass.: Peter Smith, 1963), vol. 1, 195.

[8] James M. McCaffrey, *Army of Manifest Destiny: The American Soldier in the Mexican War, 1846–1848* (New York: New York University Press, 1992), 20.

[9] Oran Perry, compiler, *Indiana in the Mexican War* (Indianapolis: William B. Burford, 1908), 83; Wylie Gettys, Jr., "'To Conquer a Peace': South Carolina and the Mexican War" (Ph.D. diss., University of South Carolina, 1974), 239.

[10] Franklin Smith diary, August 13, 1846, Mississippi Department of Archives and History, Jackson, Mississippi; John Campbell to his father, July 6, 1847, John Campbell collection, University of Virginia Library, Charlottesville, Virginia; George Ballentine, *Autobiography of an English Soldier in the United States Army* (New York: Stringer and Townshend, 1853), 49–50.

[11] Journal of Henry Edwards, Indiana Historical Society Library; Journal of John W. Fincher, Atlanta Historical Society Library; Luther Giddings, *Sketches of the Campaign in Northern Mexico in Eighteen Hundred Forty-Six and Seven By an Officer of the First Regiment of Ohio Volunteers* (New York: G. P. Putnam, 1853), 26.

[12] Ulysses S. Grant, *Personal Memoirs of U.S. Grant* (New York: Charles L. Webster and Co., 1885-86), vol. 1, 43–44.

[13] H. [D. H. Hill], "The Battles of the Rio Grande," *Southern Quarterly Review*, New Series, 2, no. 4 (November 1850), 444.

[14] Bauer, 236.

General Scott had previously designated the island of Lobos, about sixty-five miles southeast of Tampico, as a rendezvous point for troops earmarked for the landing at Veracruz. The various regiments that had recently transferred to Scott's command from General Taylor's army were to march overland to ports on the gulf coast and then sail to Lobos. New volunteer regiments being raised in the United States would sail directly for Lobos from their various marshalling points. Even though Scott's original target date of the first of the year had proven unrealistically optimistic, he confidently reported to the Secretary of War on January 26, that he hoped to start moving the troops from Taylor's army by the end of the month and expected that the landing craft and most of the rest of his needed supplies would reach Lobos by February 10.

As so often happens with plans of this magnitude, snags began to occur. There were only a finite number of ships available to transport Scott's forces, and coordinating their timely arrival proved to be quite a difficult task. Major General William Worth's division of regulars from Taylor's army had arrived at Brazos Santiago, but there were no ships waiting to take them any farther. Likewise, Brigadier General David E. Twiggs's division of regulars and General Patterson's volunteer division had reached as far as Tampico where they, too, awaited the arrival of long overdue ships. To make matters worse, shipping that was available sometimes ran into trouble. A vessel carrying volunteers from New Orleans wrecked along the Mexican coastline about forty miles south of Tampico, temporarily marooning about three hundred Louisiana volunteers. This situation caused considerable concern for their safety—as evidenced by Laidley's letter of February 12, 1847—because they were stranded in the immediate vicinity of an eight-hundred-man force under Santa Anna's brother-in-law, General Martín Perfecto de Cos.

Although the upcoming campaign for Veracruz occupied most of General Scott's time, General Taylor's army was not completely inactive. In fact, because of the way the plan for the invasion of Veracruz was developing, Taylor's situation was soon to become perilous. Scott had taken nearly all of Taylor's regulars and most of his battle-seasoned volunteers for the move against Veracruz, leaving his subordinate very unhappy. If Mexican authorities learned of this weakening of Taylor's force they might try to crush him before Scott could get a foothold at Veracruz. In fact, events unfolded that made that possibility more likely. Mexican troops ambushed and killed an American courier, and one of the dispatches they took from his body contained detailed information about the projected troop transfers. Santa Anna soon knew just how understrength Taylor's army had become.

In this letter, Laidley shows how the various logistical delays are beginning to wear on him. He is anxious for the expedition to get under way and seems to share General Scott's eagerness to get away from Brazos Santiago and to the work at hand. Near the end of this letter Laidley makes reference to his strong religious faith, which will tend to sustain him and be a continuing theme throughout the remainder of his letters home from Mexico.

Head Quarters of the Army
Brazos Santiago, Feb 12th 1847

My dear father,

Contrary to our expectations and much against our will, we still find ourselves at this place, but as we now expect to get off soon and probably will not have another opportunity of sending a letter off before we do, I will write and send by this vessel the letter I promised you and which you will be looking for.

Since my last the mist that enveloped our future operations has been dissipated and now we see our way pretty clearly.

The papers have scattered the plan of operations all over the country and of course to the enemy also, when its success depended in so great a measure on the secrecy with which it was kept. A fault, by the way, that will cost us much in all warlike operations, at all times, and most probably defeat some or many of them.

We have been expecting to get off for two weeks and made preparations for so doing at that time, but the non-arrival of transports for the troops which depends upon the winds and weather, has retarded the operations very much.

The Genl, of course, is in great anxiety of mind about it as so much depends upon the dispatch with which it is executed before the enemy has time to prepare for a vigorous defence and the yellow fever begins its ravages which are more to be feared than all that the enemy can bring against us. The Gen. is aware that his all depends upon this campaign and the delay as well as a thousand other things keeps him in a perfect fever. When he does start he will not stop till he has conquered or falls with all with him. It is Vera Cruz and the Presidency or death.

When we sail from here it will be for Lobos, where all the troops rendezvous, and thence for Antón Lizardo where we will disembark under cover of the fire from the fleet and make our way for Vera Cruz.

Santa Anna is expected there in full force as he has the most accurate and detailed account of our intentions. He will have every advantage of position and number and an obstinate conflict is expected and nothing but the superior bearing and skill of our troops will save us.

The Genl has not intimated to me what will be the nature of my duties on that occasion, whether to command a battery of heavy guns or mortars or what, and I do not expect to know till we get there.

It appears to me a very uncertain operation, so much depends upon the elements and is entirely beyond control. A norther may dissipate the fleet and scatter it to the winds, or wreck it upon the coast as a portion of the Louisiana Regiment has been already: nothing of the kind, though, seems to have entered into their calculations and our force should all arrive, would be only about thirteen thousand, the majority of which are volunteers and most of them perfectly raw.

The object of making the result for a moment doubtful, is in the least fail to impair the advantages that might result from being able to follow up a victory, I cannot imagine.

The uncertainty of our time of departure and the dislike of asking permission together with the frequent disagreeable weather has prevented me from visiting the places of interest in this vicinity. I have seen neither of the battle fields [Palo Alto

(May 8, 1846) or Resaca de la Palma (May 9, 1846)] or Mata-moros, and have consequently passed the month I have been here very stupidly.

This climate is the most abominable, most frequent and sudden changes I ever knew, and consequently I have had a cold and not been well.

However it is getting better and when we get in active service I hope to be better.

I dread the sea voyage on account of the seasickness and am afraid that I shall not be in condition to render any obstinate resistance to an enemy immediately on landing.

I have heard so much praise of Tampico that I was anxious to go there for a short time, but I find now that I shall not be able. It is spoken of as the garden of Mexico, superior to any thing that the officers have seen. The great majority of the country is a sterile, good for nothing country, not worth having, much less fighting for.

An officer, the other day, who was once a great annexation man on being asked what he now thought of it, replied that he would give Texas back to Mexico and if she would not take it he would be willing to enter into a ten years war to make her do so. This opinion seems to gain favor in the minds of many who have been out here and seen much of it. Very certain it is that they are anxious enough to leave here and get back to the states.

I have received nothing from you since I left you, but of this I do not wonder when I see how wretchedly the post office is conducted. But a great treat it is to hear from home when so far distant, and since the chance of receiving what you do write is so small, you must write the oftener.

I congratulate myself when I see the married officers so anxious, and uneasy about letters, and one could not but admit that in this kind of operations I had the advantage of him [them].

I suppose I shall not have time or opportunity to write to you again before we have met the enemy, though it may be a month or near that, first.

I am sensible that I am going surrounded by dangers of all kinds, but I am going in the discharge of my duties, and God, without whom not even a sparrow falleth to the ground, will protect me, and if I fall it will be by His will and I pray His will be done.

We have just [been] recovering from a Norther and I presume it has brought transport along with it, so we will certainly get off in a few days at the furthest.

Give my love to the family, I remain your affectionate son

<u>Theodore</u>

I presume you have heard of Lt. [John A.] Richey's [USMA 1845] being cut off with dispaches containing a detailed plan of the campaign. Also a company of Arkansas volunteers in the vicinity of Saltillo. It was supposed that a part of the Louisiana regiment that was wrecked would be surrounded and captured— not known that it was.

<u>T.</u>

Lieutenant Laidley surely mirrors the universal feelings of military men throughout our history with regard to how the press disseminated information of a sensitive military nature. It would be interesting to know how Laidley would have regarded the manner in which the U.S. military managed the media during the Persian Gulf War of 1991.

The young officer also bemoans the high percentage of volunteers in the invasion force, but in this he was mistaken. Volunteers only made up one of the three divisions slated for the operation, and some of these men had seen prior combat under General Taylor.

Laidley is more afraid of the effect of yellow fever than he is of Mexican military prowess. This attitude might be more understandable if the young officer had already experienced combat against the Mexicans and, therefore, had something upon which to base a comparison. Instead, he was full of typical American confidence. One officer who had fought through the early battles as part of General Taylor's army was no less insistent, however. Lieutenant Ulysses S. Grant was also slated to take part in the invasion of Veracruz, and he confided to his fiancee: "We will all have to get out of this part of Mexico soon or we will be caught by the yellow fever which I am ten to one more affraid of than of the Mexicans."[1]

When Laidley ascribed political aspirations to General Scott, he was not making any great philosophical deduction. Military heroes were no strangers to the White House. The military exploits of both George Washington and Andrew Jackson, both legitimate military heroes, had swept them into the White House on waves of popularity. William Henry Harrison had become the nation's ninth president due, in large part, to his claim of having slain the Indian war chief Tecumseh during the War of 1812. Already, Zachary Taylor seemed to many Americans to be a sure bet to try to recapture the White House for the Whigs in 1848.

The Arkansas volunteers to which Laidley refers were actually part of a mixed command of Arkansas and Kentucky horsemen in General Taylor's army and under the immediate command of Major Solon Borland. They had ridden out of the village of Encarnación on January 22, 1847, scouting southward looking for any sign of a Mexican military presence. Finding none, the Americans made camp for the night confident that

there were no enemy soldiers within miles of them and, therefore, they did not bother to post any sentries. The next morning, to their everlasting surprise, Colonel Miguel Andrade's 500
Mexican lancers surrounded and captured the seventy-one
Americans.

---

[1] Ulysses S. Grant to Julia Dent, February 25, 1847, in Ulysses S. Grant, *The Papers
of Ulysses S. Grant, Vol. 1, 1837–1861*, ed. John Y. Simon (Carbondale, Illinois: Southern Illinois University Press, 1967), 127.

General Scott finally tired of waiting for his transports to arrive at Brazos Santiago and sailed from there to Tampico on February 15. After a brief stay in Tampico the general left for Lobos where he arrived on the 21st. He did not find the situation there any more to his liking than elsewhere. The volunteers who had arrived were in a very poor state of preparation for war, and many of them were down with smallpox. By February 25, enough transport ships had finally arrived back at Brazos Santiago for General Worth to begin embarking the bulk of his division.

Meanwhile, the political situation, and correspondingly the military situation, had changed once again in Mexico. Santa Anna was back in power after having fallen out of favor in his native land and spending some time in exile in Havana, Cuba. Through intermediaries he had convinced President Polk that if he were allowed to pass through the American naval blockade of Mexico he would again take control of his government and very quickly work out a negotiated settlement to all the outstanding issues that had brought on the war. Wanting an end to the bloodshed, Polk took him at his word and allowed him to reenter Mexico. True to his earlier claim Santa Anna seized control of the government, but then seems to have had a change of heart with regard to relations with the United States. He took personal command of the army facing General Taylor, and he did *not* have peace talks on his mind.

The Mexican dictator set up his headquarters at San Luis Potosí and began augmenting his force with poorly equipped and untrained conscripts. He knew from captured dispatches the numerical strength of Taylor's army and would attempt to defeat him on the basis of sheer numbers. By the end of January, more than twenty thousand Mexican troops were marching northward toward the American force encamped near Saltillo. Taylor was in the inenviable position of facing the self-styled "Napoleon of the West" without many of his battle-tested troops. General Scott's proposed campaign against Veracruz had left him with no regular infantry troops, and but six volunteer infantry regiments. He did have two regular artillery regiments and two of dragoons, along with two volunteer cavalry regiments and a company of mounted Texas Rangers.

By February 19, Santa Anna was only a few miles south of the American position, but the march had been difficult. Approximately five thousand of his men had fallen out, worn down by hunger, disease, and harsh treatment. Many had died; others had deserted.

Taylor concentrated his forces at a narrow mountain pass near Hacienda San Juan de la Buena Vista and waited for the enemy to attack. The site was a good one for defense, but there was still a chance, at least in Santa Anna's mind, that a bloody battle could be avoided. He sent a message to Taylor explaining to him in very florid prose that the small American army faced overwhelming numbers and sure defeat. "But as you deserve consideration and particular esteem," the note went on, "I wish to save you from a catastrophe, and for that purpose give you this notice, in order that you may surrender at discretion, under the assurance that you will be treated with the consideration belonging to the Mexican character." Taylor was indeed outnumbered, by more than three to one, but he undoubtedly recalled the fate of Colonel James Fannin in Texas some ten years earlier. Fannin had surrendered "at discretion," and a week later he and almost all of his men were executed. General Taylor responded to the Mexican dictator's request in equally formal language, saying "I beg leave to say that I decline acceding to your request."[1]

The battle then commenced.

Lieutenant Laidley, meanwhile, was still cooling his heels at Brazos Santiago, chafing at his inactivity.

Brazos Santiago, Feb 26th '47

My dear Father

Still at Brazos! Not through any accident or anything of that kind but detained by adverse winds and wrong calculations.

We have been leaving for a month and have not gotten off yet, though I hope to get off in reality to-morrow if the wind only subsides that we may cross the bar to embark.

These winds have no regard for the plans of men and as in the present case frequently interfere materially with them.

Genl Scott first laid his plans to leave here the middle of January and now February is almost over and all of his troops have not yet left.

He cannot reach Vera Cruz before the 15th or 20th of next month which makes it very late in the season for the campaign just to begin.

Some of the officers think that it will be risky to undertake the capture of Vera Cruz at this late day for the reason that should they make anything like a determined resistance the yellow fever would take us before we could bring them to terms.

But I have no idea that Genl Scott will stop till he has made the attempt; he is bound on taking that castle cost what it may.

The Gen and staff including the Captains left here nearly two weeks since for Tampico, leaving the Subalterns to follow on with the horses; I have no doubt that he is nervous enough by this, by our non appearance, as he expected that we would have sailed long before this.

The dragoons are the only troops left yet to embark and a few days of clear weather would get them off, but about a third of the time nothing can cross the bar.

We expect to stop at Tampico for troops if they have not already all gone, so there is still a chance of our seeing that place, which I am anxious to do.

My health has not improved and I am anxious to get up in the high country as I do not expect it will till we do. This climate is certainly abominable. It is freezing and scorching in less time than I ever witnessed before.

We have just heard it rumored that Genl Taylor is expecting an attack from the Mexicans who are advancing on him. The story seems to come pretty straight and is very generally believed.

Everyone had confidence in Genl Taylor if he only had troops that he could rely on, but that he has not and has but few of any kind.

All grant that it would be Santa Anna's best course and think it very likely that it is his plan.

A very few troops could retake Matamoros and this place, thereby gaining enough provisions to last his Army for the next year.

There is but a company of forty, and no fortifications, and the whole of this line is perfectly exposed, too much so, and if we were fighting against any other nation it would be ruinous to us.

I cannot find out what we are going to do if we do take Vera Cruz, for we cannot advance to Mexico neither can we remain in it. It is to be hoped that if we take the Castle the fear of having it demolished might bring them to terms. The idea of destroying 40,000,000 of dollars would be more efficacious perhaps than killing a great number of them.

February 27th. We expect to leave tomorrow, <u>for certain</u>, I suppose. All things seem to favor.

I have not yet heard from any of you.

Give my love to all the family.

Your affectionate son
<u>Theodore</u>

Laidley still frets and fumes about being at Brazos Santiago, away from any action. The rumor mills still churn out a wide range of hearsay and gossip. The fact that the troops in this rear area still have not heard of General Taylor's victory over Santa Anna at Buena Vista illustrates how slowly news traveled.

The lieutenant seems to be having second thoughts about the wisdom of the Veracruz campaign. He may well have been thinking of the distance an army landing at the port city would still have to traverse to reach the capital. The farther into the interior the army moved, the longer would be its supply line back to the coast. This, in turn, would mean that more and more of the combat strength of the army would have to be diverted to protecting the roads.

---

[1] Report of the Secretary of War in Serial Set 503, Senate Executive Document 1, 30th Congress, 1st session, 98.

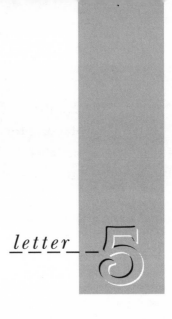

letter 5

General Scott lived up to his nickname of "Old Fuss and Feathers" as he fretted and fumed over the logistical delays he was forced to endure. By the end of February he could wait no more. The longer he waited for all of the designated troops and supplies to arrive the more time the enemy had to reinforce the defenses of Veracruz. If he did not move forward soon he would not be able to complete the campaign before the yellow fever made its deadly annual appearance along the coast. He decided to go ahead with the men he had on hand. On March 2, 1847, he ordered the troops who had assembled at Lobos to set sail for Antón Lizardo, just a few miles from his intended landing spot southeast of Veracruz.

After arriving at Antón Lizardo a few days later, Scott and most of his senior officers reconnoitered the shoreline aboard the *Petrita*, and, finding no evidence of Mexican intentions to defend it, he finalized plans for the landing. The troops would go ashore in three divisions. The first, made up of regular troops, would be under the command of Brigadier General William J. Worth, a veteran of the War of 1812 and the Seminole fighting in Florida. Volunteers would form the second division and Ma-

jor General Robert Patterson, who had left the army after serving in the War of 1812, would lead them ashore. Long-serving
Brigadier General David E. Twiggs would hold the third division, also composed of regulars, in reserve to see where it would
be needed most in case Mexican troops opposed the landing.

After postponing the landing for a day due to threatening
weather, the custom-built landing craft finally started heading
ashore with their loads of anxious soldiers late in the afternoon
of March 9, 1847. The most ambitious amphibious landing operation in the short history of the U.S. Army was under way at
last. The men in each boat strained their eyes shoreward to catch
the first sign of an enemy presence just as their descendants
would do almost a century later at such places as Tarawa, Anzio,
and Normandy. They listened intently for the boom of Mexican artillery or the crack of musket fire. To the surprise of many
and the relief of all there was no sign of an enemy presence on
shore. As soon as the first troops reached the shore the sailors
manning the oars of the surfboats began pulling back toward
the fleet for another load of soldiers. The lack of armed Mexican resistance to the landing obviously made things much easier
than they might have been, and the boats shuttled troops and
supplies ashore for the next five and a half hours. By eleven
o'clock that night, approximately 8,600 men had been put
ashore.

General Scott, of course, realized that getting his army off
the ships and onto solid ground was only the first step in reduc-
ing the defenses of Veracruz. On paper, Veracruz presented a
very formidable obstacle to any attacking force. Fifteen-foot high
masonry walls punctuated with periodic artillery positions surrounded the city. A determined force, well supplied with food,
water, and ammunition, should be able to keep any attacker at
bay for some time. Even if the Americans were able to breach
the city walls there was the additional fortress, or castle, called

San Juan d'Ulúa about a half mile offshore on Gallega Reef. The castle's 135 cannons, many of them of the most up-to-date design, could make actual occupation of the city impossible.

There was some light skirmishing as the Americans began moving to encircle the city on the land side. Progress in completing siege lines was slow, however, because of the time it took to ferry supplies ashore. The men would need draft animals to haul the heavy siege guns into position. These guns would then need considerable quantities of heavy shot. Food for both men and animals must constantly be on hand.

Tampico, Mexico
March 11th, 1847

My dear Father

I have bare time enough to drop you a few lines from this place to let you know of my whereabouts and to communicate what I hear of Genl Taylor's success, though you may, perhaps, be better acquainted with the details by the time that you receive this, than anything I can tell you.

We left Brazos on the 3[d] of this month and after a week's sailing reached this place last night having had a long and tedious passage tho in other respects a very pleasant [one]. We expected to take in troops at this place but find that all of the troops have left, that Genl Scott has left Lobos and proceeded on to Vera Cruz, so we leave early this morning with all possible haste to get thru, if possible, before he takes that City as it is thought he will not meet with a very strong resistance. We shall, doubtless, find his Army on shore waiting, perhaps, for horses to move his guns against the wall of the city.

We learn here from the Mexicans that Santa Anna moved against Genl Taylor with about 20,000 men who retreated from Saltillo to Monterey, and two battles were fought on the 23$^{\underline{d}}$ and 24$^{\underline{th}}$ in which the Mexican General claims to have repulsed the American forces with a loss of Americans of 2,000 men, three guns and ten stand of colors, though he deemed it prudent to retreat for want of water and provisions. That the battles were fought with great obstinacy on both sides the Mexicans being encouraged by the expectation of taking from our forces the provisions which they so much needed.

What will be the true story when the other side is known, we may judge by allowing for Mexican bombast and exaggerating. It is supposed that Genl Taylor with not five thousand has repulsed some 20,000.

This is a beautiful town indeed. As we approached it coming up the river it presented as pleasant a scene as I ever beheld. It is situated on the left bank, on a rising slope and is seen to advantage on an approach from the south. The houses are mostly of one story built of stone, occasionally a two storied one, flat roof and parapet walls, grated windows, and the windows all opening and fastening inwards.

The streets are paved with stone, sloping inwards and no gutters. I have not had an opportunity of seeing as much as I would like as it was nearly dark when we arrived. It is pretty strongly fortified by our forces and is now garrisoned by about a thousand men, mostly volunteers, and if any kind of force should come against it, with the present discipline it would stand but a short time.

I, of course, enquired about Mrs. Chase on my arrival, and the romance that the papers had thrown around her name for her heroic conduct war [was?] rather dispelled by the description that was given me.

She may be seen by any one, a great strapping Irish [English] woman selling tape and other like articles in a shop on a public corner of the plaza.

But I must conclude as it is nearly day and I leave as soon as it is light.

Give my love to all. I remain,

Yours affectionately,
Theodore

As with most rumors in war time, there was some—but only *some*—truth to the rumor of General Taylor's success at Buena Vista. His force of approximately 4,600 men was indeed outnumbered by Santa Anna, who sent an estimated 15,000 men into battle. Once again, it was the American artillery that helped win the contest. After two days of fierce fighting, Santa Anna decided to lead his men south again. The Americans lost about fourteen percent of their strength in killed, wounded, and missing. The much larger Mexican force lost almost a fourth of its men. American losses were 272 killed, 387 wounded, and six missing. Santa Anna admitted to losing 591 killed, 1,048 wounded, and 1,894 missing.[1]

Lieutenant Laidley has obviously overcome his slight tinge of doubt, expressed near the end of his letter of February 26, 1847, about the ability of Scott's force to capture Veracruz.

---

[1] K. Jack Bauer, *The Mexican War* (New York: Macmillan, 1974), 209, 217.

Skirmishes with Mexican forces did not prevent General Twiggs's men from reaching the coast north of Veracruz on March 13, thereby completing the encirclement of the city. General Scott hoped to be able to exert enough pressure to force a surrender without having to resort to an actual infantry assault upon the fortified city. He had no doubt that an attack would be successful in compelling a surrender, but at a cost in American lives that he was unwilling to pay.

Siege work was slow, and stormy weather prevented American sailors from landing necessary supplies as fast as was hoped. The sun finally made an appearance again on March 17, and work began in earnest to prepare protected battery positions for Scott's heavy siege guns. By March 22, he was ready to give the order for the bombardment to commence. First, he sent a message asking the Mexican commander, Brigadier General Juan Morales, to surrender the city peacefully. Morales of course refused, and Scott's seven ten-inch mortars began lobbing shells over the city's walls late that afternoon. Offshore, American ships began shelling the city in concert.

Although General Scott did not have all the heavy artillery he believed necessary for the work at hand, he was not limited to the short, squatty, high trajectory mortars to do his work. Even as these guns began lobbing their shells into the city, boat crews were landing six heavy naval cannons for use against the city walls. Engineer Captain Robert E. Lee had laid out the battery position for the naval guns about seven hundred yards from the city, and by the morning of March 24 the sailors assigned as gun crews added their fire to that of the mortars.

The defenders of Veracruz did not simply sit idly by while the American artillery pounded their city into ruins. Mexican artillery responded as best it could, but the damage it caused among the American ranks was not extensive. Outside the city, there continued to be skirmishes of varied intensities as Mexican reinforcements sought to find a weak spot in the American siege lines through which to reach the beleaguered garrison. Rumors also appeared that said that Santa Anna, having returned from tangling with General Taylor at Buena Vista, was now approaching Veracruz from the west with a 6,000-man relief force.

This rumor added a degree of urgency to American plans. Scott still believed that a siege would be less costly in American lives, but if a strong force appeared in his rear his army might very well be caught in a vise from which there was no ready escape. He began making plans for a three-pronged frontal assault to capture the city before significant numbers of enemy reinforcements could arrive.

Happily for the Americans, General Morales heeded the consensus of his subordinates, which was to surrender before the American artillery killed even more of the city's defenders and civilian inhabitants. The bombardment stopped on the morning of March 26 and the terms of capitulation were finalized the next day. Morales not only surrendered the Veracruz garrison but also those troops stationed within San Juan d'Ulúa. The defeated soldiers would not have to go to prison camps in the United States. Instead they signed paroles promising not to take up arms against the United States again in this war. Mexican officers retained their personal property, such as side arms and horses, and the formal surrender ceremony was scheduled for March 29.

Camp Washington, near Vera Cruz
March 27th 1847

My dear Father

I understand that the "Princeton" sails to-morrow with the news of the surrender of the city and castle together with all the troops munitions etc.[1] As you will, doubtless, feel anxious to know of my safety and everything connected with it I hasten to give you a short sketch of the operations.

It is now late and I have been out in the trenches all day, and just got back, so do not be surprised at my brevity which I promise to make up for at some more leisure time.

I landed here on the 17th and found that the army had landed on the 9th and were busily engaged in getting things on shore.

They met with no resistance whatever in landing which they effected just beyond the reach of the guns of the castle. The city was immediately surrounded, its communications cut off and everything prepared for a seige of the place. My department was busy in getting the guns and ammunition and other things in preparation, and had them placed in their positions.

Last Monday the 22d we opened the fire from seven mortars on the city and the enemy at the same time bringing everything to play on us, and such a hot time I never saw before and never wish to see again. The air was rent with the whistling of balls, the roaring of our own mortars, and the bustle and confusion incident to such an exciting time. The bombardment continued with but little interruption, we adding as fast as possible to the numbers of our mortars and guns, till yesterday when they sounded a parley, which after a good deal of talk resulted in the unconditional surrender of the town and castle, the officers and soldiers being taken prisoners of war.

We have not yet marched in the city but understand that we will to-morrow; we hear that it is very much shattered by our firing and the loss of life and property on their side has been immense whereas on ours it has been inconsiderable.

Two officers killed and ten wounded, some 5 or 6 men killed and some 12 or 15 wounded. One naval officer and several seamen killed.

I was in the hottest of it, in the discharge of my duties and was near by when a shell exploded and killed one and wounded others. The sight was terrible and with grateful feelings is it that I return my thanks to Almighty God for the preservation of my life through the dangers to which I have been exposed.

My department has had hard work to perform and the officers have performed it creditably.

It is very unexpected and almost incredible that we should have taken so strong a place as the castle with so little loss and in so short a time.

It is thought that a want of provisions forced them into terms sooner than anything else.

The victory has not yet been announced to the Army by general orders, and I only write this lest the "Princeton" might get off without my sending you something by it.

I have not yet heard the first word from you since I left. What we will do no one pretends to know, though all expect to move on to Jalapa.

I am in hopes that this with the recent victories of Genl Taylor will make them come to terms and thus bring about a peace. The destructions of their Castle, a very perfect work, would have more influence than most anything else. But it is impossible to foretell what course a Mexican will pursue and it would be vain to attempt it. I sincerely wish that a peace may be brought about and let us quit this brutal, demoralizing work.

I have seen enough already, and am quite satisfied. When I have time I will tell you more about the city when I have seen it close and have more time. To-morrow is Sunday, but few know it, it is not distinguishable from other days; I long to get back where it is otherwise.

Join me in praising God for my preservation and that we may yet meet again.

My love to all.

Yours affectionately
<u>Theodore</u>

Finally, Laidley had reached the war. The relatively light casualties incurred by the Americans made his initiation into combat a little less shocking than might have been the case.[2] And even though there is nothing in his earlier letters that betrays an eagerness to experience war—or to "see the elephant"—the comparatively minor human carnage he saw outside Veracruz seems to have satisfied any unuttered desires to be a warrior.

[1] The U.S.S. *Princeton* was a four-year-old, single-screw steam warship mounting one 8-inch shell gun and twelve 42-pounder cannonades. K. Jack Bauer, *Surfboats and Horse Marines: U.S. Naval Operations in the Mexican War, 1846–1848* (Annapolis: United States Naval Institute Press, 1969), 257.

[2] Laidley's report of American casualties is somewhat less than official figures of two officers and nine men killed and fifty-one officers and men wounded, three fatally. Richard H. Coolidge, *Statistical Report of the Sickness and Mortality in the Army of the United States compiled from the Records of the Surgeon General's Office; Embracing a Period of Sixteen Years, From January, 1839, to January 1855* (Washington, D.C.: A.O.P. Nicholson, 1856), 613, 618.

letter 7

Cannon fire again broke out near Veracruz on the morning of March 29, but it was only Mexican cannons firing a final salute as their flags came down. The Mexicans of the garrison, having signed their paroles, marched out from the city, stacked their weapons, and turned over all other government property before traveling inland. Victorious American soldiers then occupied the city and the castle and raised the Stars and Stripes over both.

As the Americans entered the city, they saw for the first time just how effective their big cannons and mortars had been. Many buildings were damaged, some had burned. The unburied bodies of dead animals of all sizes littered the roadways and added to the unpleasant aroma of the rotting garbage that was routinely thrown into the streets by the inhabitants. Open gutters in the middle of the streets theoretically served as sewers, while large buzzard-like birds scavenged through this debris at their leisure. One of the newly arrived American officers delicately described the smell as "very unlike cologne."[1]

Not all of the battle damage in Veracruz was structural. There were also a number of human casualties. Although the exact

53

number is indeterminable, there were probably at least a hundred soldiers and a like number of civilians killed by incoming American artillery shells. The U.S. soldiers expected to inflict this kind of damage on the enemy army, but most were saddened by the evidence of so many civilian deaths. Captain Robert E. Lee captured this sentiment in a letter to his wife: "My heart bled for the inhabitants. The [Mexican] soldiers I did not care so much for, but it was terrible to think of the women and children."[2]

General Scott now had his base of operations for the overland march to Mexico City, but a lot of work remained before such a move would be possible. Before the Americans could use the city as a supply depot for further operations they would have to repair much of the damage they had wrought. And they would have to stockpile tons of supplies to support the next step in the campaign.

General Scott named General Worth to be the temporary military governor of Veracruz with responsibility of cleaning up the city. He got right to work on the problems, hiring about two hundred local men to clean up the battle damage and the ordinary filth in the streets. According to the medical beliefs of the day, the miasma that arose from the rotting garbage and animal carcasses that littered the streets was the basic cause of all manner of tropical fevers. Even though this was erroneous, the vigorous cleanup campaign that ensued did remove much of the potential breeding areas of the mosquitoes that *did* carry disease.

Scott was anxious to continue the military campaign and seemed to think that Quartermaster General Thomas Jesup had grossly overestimated the needs of his army for such a move. Jesup calculated that a 25,000-man army would require over nine thousand wagons and almost twice as many pack animals to move the almost fifteen hundred tons of supplies it would require. This included everything from food and forage for the soldiers and animals to three hundred bottles of ink and five thousand writing quills.[3]

Although the rumors of Santa Anna arriving with troops to reinforce the Veracruz garrison had proven false, he *was* preparing to dispute the further passage of American soldiers into the interior of Mexico. From Mexico City he organized a force which he called the Army of the East whose goal was to keep the Americans from penetrating any farther than the city of Jalapa. On April 2, he left the capital to take personal command of this force.

In Veracruz, Scott, too, had finalized his campaign plans and the advance guard of his army left the city headed west, also on April 2.

Vera Cruz, Mexico
April 2[d] 1847

My dear Father

I feel somewhat at a loss what to write to you about the seige, knowing that you will see much in the papers about it, lest I should tell you what you have already seen over and again.

You know that we threw up entrenchments about 800 yards from the walls of the city planted our batteries and threw some three thousand ten inch shells, which exploded in the city, besides other shells and solid shot. It was the duty of the Ordnance officer stationed in the trenches to have the cartridges made, the shells loaded and the fuzes cut to the right length so that they should burst at the right times. He had to visit the different batteries to see what was wanted and direct the operations of all, so although we did not actually fire the pieces, the important part, that upon which the accuracy of fire depended, devolved upon us, and of course, the credit of the bombardment is due to the ordnance officers, and they get it, too, from the greater part of the army where it is understood. I do not know how it will appear in the newspapers, for an Artillery officer had the general direction, nominal and also made the report so we do not expect much from his hands, knowing the jealousy with which they view us.

Last Monday the Mexicans marched out of the city and Castle, laid down their arms and left on their parole.

Our troops marched in at the same time raised our flag at the principal fort and the castle when the navy and the foreign vessels all saluted it as it went up.

A pretty sight it was to see the stars and stripes waving over these strong holds where so short time before the Mexican flag seemed to defy our utmost efforts.

I rode through the city and truly it was a sorry sight to see the desolation that the shells had made among the houses. The fragments were lying in every direction, the streets were barricaded, defences of sandbags were everywhere thrown up, the city seemed deserted, and the streets echoed the tramp of our horses. The city has an antique appearance, large churches with steeples or domes, built with considerable architectural pretensions, the houses low, with flat roofs and parapet walls, altogether different from any of our cities. The streets well paved, but most abominably filthy—they seem to be the receptacle of all the filth of the place, vultures being the only scavengers which they know. It strikes every one at first sight—no wonder that they have the yellow fever in Vera Cruz. You can form no idea of its extent; most offensive odors salute you where ever you go within its walls.

It is a pretty strong place and if it had been defended with any vigor, it would have cost us dearly to have taken it, but they are a great set of cowards as all of the battles have sufficiently proved. The French consul told us that the gunners had to be tied to the pieces before they capitulated. They never made a single sortie upon our trenches or otherwise molest[ed] us in the night except by an occasional shell. About 4,000 men marched out of the city who had given their word not to bear arms against us during the war.

I have been all through the Castle, the famous San Juan d'Ulúa, and a truly strong place it is. And then to think we have obtained possession of it without the least exertion, without striking a blow. It surpasses all calculations, no one dreamed of it. Every one thought we would have to throw them some 75,000 shells first and we were preparing to do it as soon as we had possession of the city—but we were saved the expense and we have it without being in the least harmed[?] by the battling of cannon.

It is very strong, has mounted in it, now, 130 guns, some of the largest calibre, many of them made by our own people. The magazines filled with any amount of ammunition and everything ready for a most obstinate resistance. We are now getting ready to march into the interior. An expedition has gone to Alvarado which we expect will hasten our departure as it is expected it will bring us means of transportation which we are waiting for.

I am fortunate in having a pleasant mess of four ordnance officers and we get along very pleasantly, have every comfort, perhaps no officers have more than us. Our chief, Capt. [Benjamin] Huger, is very much of a gentleman and does everything to make us comfortable in his power.[4] We hope to continue together as it will [be] much more agreeable for all parties, though there was some talk of my going to [Maj.] Gen. [Robert] Paterson which I trust may blow over and be heard of no more.

We will hardly get off for ten days yet to come, so many preparations are to be made. It will be refreshing to get on the high grounds for it is hot enough here now and growing hotter every day.

'Tis getting late, so I will bid you good night.

Your affectionate son
Theodore

⁂ • ⁂

Laidley's initial description of his duties during the siege do, indeed, seem to overlap those of the artillery officers, and it is no surprise that there was some intraservice rivalry.

Laidley was not alone in his denigration of the fighting spirit of Mexican troops. Their suspected lack of patriotism was a subject much remarked upon by American soldiers. A Virginia volunteer officer, for example, thought that enemy soldiers displayed "a degree of cowardice & a want of patriotism perfectly incomprehensible to the sons of the Old Dominion, and the fact has convinced me, or rather strengthened the conviction already entertained, that the Anglo-Saxon race possess more of the higher qualities which ennoble man than any other on the face of the earth."[5]

Examination of the fortress of San Juan d'Ulúa only seemed to reinforce the low opinion of Mexican will to fight. Another American officer also mentioned that several of the cannons were American-made; in fact, some had been cast at West Point Foundry, directly across the Hudson River from the Military Academy. Others came from France and Spain.[6]

Laidley's stated reluctance to serve under General Patterson is the first instance in these letters of his own anti-volunteer bias.

---

[1] William Austine to his brother, April 1, 1847, in "America's First D-Day: The Veracruz Landing of 1847," ed. James M. McCaffrey, *Military History of the West*, 25, no. 1 (Spring 1995), 67.

[2] Robert E. Lee to his wife, ca. March 24, 1847, in Philip Van Doren Stern, *Robert E. Lee: The Man and the Soldier* (New York: Bonanza Books, 1963), 78.

[3] K. Jack Bauer, *The Mexican War* (New York: Macmillan, 1974), 259.

[4] Benjamin Huger (1805–1877), of South Carolina, graduated from the Military Academy at West Point eighth in his class of thirty-seven in 1825. During the Civil War, he would rise to the rank of major general in the Confederate Army. George W. Cullum, *Biographical Register of Officers and Graduates of the U.S. Military Academy at West Point, New York since its Establishment in 1802*, ed. Wirt Robinson, Supplement Volume VI-A (Saginaw, Michigan: Seemann and Peters, 1920), 21; Ezra J. Warner, *Generals in Gray: Lives of the Confederate Commanders* (Baton Rouge: Louisiana State University Press, 1959), 143–44.

[5] T. H. Towner to his father, April 14, 1847, Benjamin Towner papers, Duke University Library, Durham, North Carolina.

[6] Robert Anderson, *An Artillery Officer in the Mexican War 1846–7*, ed. Eba Anderson Lawton (New York and London: G. P. Putnam's Sons, 1911), 106.

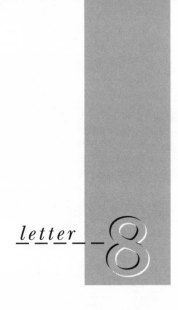

The yellow fever season would soon begin in the coastal areas so General Scott was anxious to move as many of his troops as possible out of Veracruz and into the higher elevations. He chose the city of Jalapa, almost a mile above sea level and about seventy-five miles inland from Veracruz, as a likely place from which to escape the heat and fever of the coast. Of course, Santa Anna also realized the effect that fever could have on an invading force and was determined to prevent the Americans from reaching the more temperate climate.

On April 2, Scott sent Lieutenant Colonel William S. Harney with a force of dragoons to reconnoiter the road to Jalapa. Within a week Generals Twiggs and Patterson had set their divisions in motion, and General Worth's men only waited for additional wagons and pack animals before they would begin to march. During that same interval, Santa Anna selected Cerro Gordo, about five miles east of Jalapa, as the place where he would stop the American advance.

Vera Cruz, Mexico April 11ᵗʰ, 1847

My dear Father

A rather unexpected order to march, on short notice, makes me write in more of a hurry than I wish, and I expect less satisfactorily than you would wish.

The advance marched on the 8ᵗʰ, and for fear that they might be in want of some large guns to tear down entrenchments, barricades or other obstacles we start off to-morrow with a section of heavy guns, consisting of two 24 pdrs. and one seige 8 inch Howitzer, with one small mortar.

The Genl [Scott] leaves also to-morrow for the head of the column and will be followed by [Brig.] Genl [William J.] Worth as soon as the means of transportation are furnished.

There are rumors, with what grounds, or what credence is to be given to them, I do not know, that Santa Anna is approaching, with a large force, this side of Jalapa, and I suppose it is with a view of meeting him that such haste is made in moving on.[1] I suppose it would be the best thing possible if we could meet him and whip him soundly, then perhaps we might have peace, for until that does happen it seems the[y] are not contented. The issue of any battle is no longer regarded as doubtful, by those who have seen the manner in which they fight at other places heretofore.

We have not heard that the advance had met any obstacles as yet, though it was expected that they would at Puente del Rey, some forty miles from this place, where they have a fort that guards the National Bridge. I was ordered to march with Genl Patterson on the 9ᵗʰ, but our Captain objecting to having his force so split up, succeeded in having the order countermanded.

I was in hopes we would not be separated but permitted to march altogether, it would be so much more pleasant for all of us, but another officer of the Ordnance and I go with this section, leaving the rest to follow as soon as a sufficient number of teams can be furnished to haul the rest or another section.

It is about time that we were leaving the "tierras calientes," as they call it, the hot lands; though the yellow fever has not yet made its appearance among the troops or in the city, still sickness of some kinds, fevers or the disease of the country, is pretty common and becoming more so every day. The volunteers not knowing how to take care of them, thus suffer the most and deaths among them are becoming more common.

The city is very much improved in cleanliness, though I should still dislike very much to remain within its walls and take my chance of being sick.

Though an Ordnance officer is very much needed to remain at the city, but Capt has determined that no one shall remain, but has hired a person to remain and take care of the Ordnance property that will be left behind which will be very great. We are all, of course, highly delighted that none of us have to remain.

Ordnance officers are in great demand, there being requisitions upon us for officers that we could not fill for the marching column; in fact there are no officers who have had to work harder than we; and when the town was taken our labors instead of being over as was the case with most of the troops were as arduous as ever if not more so, and have continued so. Last Sunday was the first rest we have had, or the first day that at all appeared like <u>sunday</u>, on others we have had to work as other days. What a relief it will be to be once more able to keep it as it should be done and once more enjoy the privileges of attending the services of the Church, of joining in her prayers and praises.

The Genl and a number of the officers attended the Cathedral last Sunday, Easter Sunday—but the majority were prompted by curiosity and as I do not admit that a proper motive for going to church, and as I could not take part in the services, it being all Greek to me, I preferred remaining at home.

We are anxiously looking for news from the States, it has been so long since we heard; for my part I have not received a letter since I have been in the country, and I am in hopes the next mail will bring me one.

I do not know where our next halt will be, but when we do so I shall write at the first opportunity.

Give my love to all. Adieu.

Your affectionate son
<u>Theodore</u>

Laidley again shows his concern for maintaining his health and the hope that he will not have to remain as part of the American garrison at Veracruz while the rest of the army moves inland. Yellow fever had not yet made its annual appearance, but it would not be long in arriving and would undoubtedly wreak havoc on any large concentration of troops. The unfortunate victim first might notice a feverish feeling, soon accompanied by chills. His head would ache, and soon the pain would move into the joints of his arms, legs, and back. As the disease progressed he would experience vomiting and constipation. Soon, internal hemorrhaging would darken the vomit, giving rise to the Mexican nickname for the disease, *vomito negro*, or black vomit. The aspect that caused others to call this sickness *yellow* fever was that in advanced stages, the body greatly reduced its excretion of bile, and that caused the skin to assume a yellowish tinge. Since yellow fever shared so many of its symptoms, at least in the early stages, with other illnesses, medical men often misdiagnosed it inadvertently.

General Scott assigned Doctor John B. Porter to set up a hospital in the occupied city as soon as possible so he and his staff would be ready to treat the inevitable yellow fever patients. Porter selected San Francisco, the Franciscan convent, for this purpose. It was situated near the waterfront and was well ventilated to make maximum use of the sea breezes. The new hospital's airiness was about the only asset it had. There was virtually nothing in the way of furniture. There were no operating tables, no beds for patients, no cooking facilities, and no utensils of any kind.[2]

Making the situation still worse was the terrible lack of qualified medical personnel. Army doctors, generally, were quite capable, but there were not enough of them to spare. Most had to accompany their regiments westward. The army then resorted to hiring civilian doctors to take up the slack. Unfortunately, some of these men were mere hacks from the streets of New Orleans or from the civilian populace of Veracruz itself. Competent nurses and hospital stewards were also in short supply. These men were often on detached duty from their regiments, and the reason that they were detached in the first place is because their officers wanted to get rid of them.

In spite of the lack of precise knowledge as to the causes of the various tropical diseases that were so common in the army, preventive measures were encouraged. Dr. E. H. Barton, one of the hired doctors, encouraged the soldiers to abstain from rich foods and intoxicating drink. He believed that overindulgence in these areas placed undue stress on the digestive system and thereby laid it wide open to disease. He also advised them to stay indoors and out of the tropical heat if possible, particularly between the hours of 7 A.M. and 2 P.M. They should avoid drafty areas and should not allow themselves out in the rain. Realizing that it would be impossible for the entire garrison to stay in the shade all day, he tempered this advice with the suggestion that those who absolutely could not avoid such exposure should be extra careful about their dress. He advised them to layer their clothing, with flannel for the innermost garments. After all, he warned, they should "rather be too warm than too cool." If none of this worked, the soldier should see the doctor at the first indication of sickness.[3]

The treatment of those who did contract yellow fever was imprecise at best, at least by modern standards. Most medical men agreed that quinine was essential in combating the disease, even though later studies have proved it to have virtually no effect. Doctors also prescribed liberal amounts of calomel— mercury chloride—and frequent salt water enemas to ease the sufferer's constipation. Doctors often gave the victims small amounts of morphine to help them sleep at the end of a day of such treatment. In spite of the best efforts of army doctors and those civilian medical men who signed on as contract surgeons, approximately one out of every four men who contracted yellow fever died.

Laidley's physical well being was not the only aspect of his health that concerned him. He also was vitally interested in his spiritual welfare. Throughout history, the army has seldom been viewed as a place for pious, reflective, churchgoing men, although the army certainly did not endorse such a negative image. Indeed, the Second Article of War "earnestly recommended to all officers and soldiers diligently to attend Divine service," but the fact that the total number of chaplains assigned to the army was not to exceed twenty—a number arrived at before the wartime buildup of troops—meant that there were many locations where church attendance was physically impossible. When no chaplains were on duty, regulations recommended that the men attend civilian churches in their vicinity.[4]

In Mexico, however, this produced yet another difficulty. Virtually all the civilian churches in Mexico were Roman Catholic, but only a small minority of American soldiers practiced that faith. There was a considerable anti-Catholic sentiment in the United States in the mid-1840s, and the letters of many American soldiers contain indignant references to the "priest ridden" Mexican society. Although Lieutenant Laidley does not express such negative sentiments in his letters, his West Point classmate D. H. Hill was quite explicit with his opinion. After having attended Mass, Hill wrote in his diary that "the mummery of the service would have been laughable had it not been so melancholy to reflect that 'twas an attempt at the worship of God."[5]

---

[1] The rumors were true. Santa Anna had returned to Mexico City from his defeat at Buena Vista in February. After assuming control of the government, he raised more recruits, forced a large loan from the Catholic Church, and headed eastward on April 2. K. Jack Bauer, *The Mexican War* (New York: Macmillan, 1974), 260–61.

[2] John B. Porter, "Medical and Surgical Notes of Campaigns in the War with Mexico, during the Years 1845, 1846, 1847, and 1848," *The American Journal of the Medical Sciences* 26 (October 1853), 312.

[3] E. H. Barton, "Means of Preserving Health at Vera Cruz," *The Boston Medical and Surgical Journal* 36, no. 24 (1847), 484.

[4] *General Regulations for the Army of the United States, 1841* (Washington, D.C.: 1841), 34.

[5] Archibald W. Burns journal, Duke University Library, Durham, North Carolina; Wyatt B. Stapp to Sarah Jane Berry, May 16, 1848, Filson Club, Louisville, Kentucky; Daniel H. Hill diary, September 6, 1846, University of North Carolina Library, Chapel Hill, North Carolina.

letter 9

An American scouting party discovered the Mexican defenses near Cerro Gordo on April 12. It was potentially a very strong position. The terrain was rugged and Santa Anna had posted troops and artillery batteries in the hills on both sides of the road. These were not, however, well trained, seasoned veterans. Most of the Mexican soldiers in the newly raised Army of the East were recent conscripts who now faced an American army that had not lost a major battle in this war.

After the American reconnaissance initially revealed the presence of the enemy position, several days went by as General Scott consolidated the rest of his army. Lieutenant Pierre G. T. Beauregard reported the possibility of getting around the enemy left and into their rear on April 12, and three days later Captain Robert E. Lee not only confirmed his observation but reported the existence of a fairly passable trail leading in that direction.

Finally, on the morning of April 17, General Twiggs's division began to move. Scott hoped that this part of his army would be able to get into the rear of Santa Anna's position and cut the road, thereby trapping the Mexicans between two American forces. Alert Mexican soldiers spotted Twiggs's men before they were able to get completely around them, and a sharp engagement ensued. The Americans clambered up a hill and pushed the defenders off, but spirited Mexican resistance kept them from repeating the feat at another nearby elevation. Darkness stopped the fighting for the day.

General Scott's battle plan for the 18th called for Twiggs, with reinforcements, to continue trying to force his way into the enemy's rear to cut the road. At the same time, Major General Gideon Pillow, a close personal friend of President Polk, was to lead his brigade of volunteers against three Mexican artillery batteries on the opposite side of the road. The regulars fought splendidly that day, driving the Mexicans from their positions and capturing hundreds of them. Pillow, however, exhibited a complete lack of military competence. His men, though individually valiant, were victimized by inadequate advance planning and suffered fearful losses as a result. Luckily for the volunteers, the Mexicans who had been inflicting such a pounding on them began to fear that Twiggs might indeed get in behind them so they broke off the fight in this sector and began to retreat.

By the middle of the day Santa Anna and many of his troops were in headlong flight to avoid capture. Nevertheless, American troops did capture over three thousand enemy troops that day, including about two hundred officers. American losses were relatively light. Of the approximately 8,500 men engaged, only 63 were killed and another 368 wounded.[1]

The day after the battle the American army, once again triumphant, marched into Jalapa.

❖ • ❖

Pass of the Sierra Gordo, Mexico,
April 19<u>th</u> 1847

My dear Father

I wrote to you last as I was starting from Vera Cruz which place we left on the 13th with a train of five heavy carriages with guns &c and trailers[?] of ammunition forage &c. As the Army had stopped at this place and was waiting for us to come forward before attacking the enemy who had strongly fortified the hills commanding the road for a long distance, and had determined to stop us if possible, we pushed forward with all the despatch that we were able; we got here on the morning of 17<u>th</u> and immediately got to work to place two large guns in position. I was sent off to place an 8 inch Howitzer in rear of the one of the enemies batteries to annoy him while the assaulting party came up in front. We had to pull it by hand for two and a half miles over the worst road you can imagine which took us all night and part of the next morning. About 9 o'clock the assaulting party under Genl Twiggs stormed the enemies battery placed on a very high hill which they drove the enemy from with great loss.

At the same time Genl Pillow with a division of Volunteers made an attempt to carry a battery by storm but failed, his men being repulsed, and could not take it. In strength it could not be compared with the one . . . carried by Genl Twiggs. Genl Worth formed the reserve and was not called upon to do anything the attacking party being so successful.

I opened my piece and fired it only eight times at the battery which Genl Pillow attacked, when it seeing the hill carried between him and Jalapa, and all hopes of escaping cut off hoisted the white flag and the work was over. The musketry fire where Genl Twiggs was, was very hot and the battle was fiercely contested. It is astonishing to see how the men climbed the steep hill in face of the enemy and succeeded in driving them from it. Nothing cannot compare with this in the obstacles overcome and none of the battles yet fought, in the results is of half the importance. Genl Santa Anna commanded but left very early in the morning before we made the attack.

We took five Generals prisoners—Eleven colonels and some four thousand prisoners—one General was killed on the field. Genls [José Joaquín de] Herrera and [Rómulo de] la Vega are among those taken. Genl [James] Shields of our side was mortally wounded, the Rifle Regiment suffered severely.

The number of killed and wounded is not known, though it is very large, not so large as the enemies.

A good many of the enemy escaped by crossing the river, the number not known. A party followed them closely took some prisoners and the whole army is moving on. Twiggs has gone on and Worth moved this morning. Santa Anna's carriage and private property was all taken, even his dinner and his liquors. A large amount of money 120,000$ was also captured.

The battle reflects the greatest credit on our troops and upon the plan of attack. There is in the battle that shows a little of the science of war. They had rendered it impossible to go along the road so we cut another road around their strong holds and attacked them in rear, turned their positions. We took some 12 or 15 pieces of artillery with ammunition of all kinds. The soldiers behaved well toward the wounded Mexicans, lying side by side and attended by the same surgeon, and the cry of "agua" (water) did not go unheeded though it was scarce and they had so short time before been contending so fiercely together.

The country here is mountainous and beautiful indeed, when I get a little time I will tell you more about it, but we are going to march on and I have merely time to scratch this off to tell you that I am safe, thanks to God for his goodness, and to give you some of the particulars of the battle—a few more such I think will conquer a piece [peace]—I am in hopes so—the horrors of war one can not understand until you have seen it. The wail of the dead march and the volleys of musketry tell of the sad duties that are now going on. Let us pray earnestly that God will bring to a speedy termination this terrible destruction of life and that peace may again reign undisturbed.

My love to all

Your affectionate son Theodore

(great health)

⁑ • ⁑

Laidley could not resist belittling the failed efforts of the volunteers in the Battle of Cerro Gordo, pointing out that the enemy in their front was not nearly as strong as that facing General Twiggs's regulars. Actually, his invective was misdirected. The volunteer soldiers fought valiantly in most of the battles in which they participated, but at Cerro Gordo they had the misfortune of being under the command of General Pillow, and his grasp of things military was sadly deficient.

Though Laidley's estimate of the number of casualties on each side was not entirely accurate, the results of this battle were indeed impressive. One of the many Mexican officers captured was General de la Vega. In fact, he found himself a prisoner of war for the second time in less than a year. American dragoons had captured him in the midst of the fierce fighting at Resaca de la Palma on May 9, 1846.[2]

Laidley was mistaken as to the lethality of General Shields's wound. The plucky Irish-born officer eventually recovered, but losses in the Rifle Regiment were quite heavy. Eleven of the sixty-four Americans killed in this battle were from this one regiment, as well as sixty-three of the 353 total wounded.[3]

Some Illinois volunteers made a capture after this battle that Laidley had not learned of when he wrote this letter. It was an artificial leg owned by none other than the Mexican dictator himself. Santa Anna had lost the lower portion of his left leg during a short war with France in 1838 and was apparently in such haste to escape from the victorious Americans at Cerro Gordo that he left it behind.[4]

---

[1] K. Jack Bauer, *The Mexican War* (New York: Macmillan, 1974), 268.

[2] Bauer, 268.

[3] Richard H. Coolidge, *Statistical Report of the Sickness and Mortality in the Army of the United States compiled from the Records of the Surgeon General's Office; Embracing a Period of Sixteen Years, From January 1839, to January, 1855* (Washington, D.C.: A.O.P. Nicholson, 1856), 613, 618.

[4] David Nevin, *The Mexican War* (Alexandria, Virginia: Time-Life Books, 1978), 150.

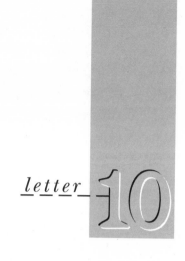

letter 10

After the battle at Cerro Gordo, and the headlong flight of the shattered Mexican army, American regimental surgeons and their assistants roamed over the battlefield collecting the wounded soldiers from both sides for treatment. In spite of their humanitarian efforts, however, the primitive state of medical knowledge at the time doomed many of the wounded to death from infection. Doctors appropriated several nearby peasant huts for their field hospital, but the conditions were hardly conducive to good health. The walls were often nothing more than cane poles stuck vertically into the ground and tied together, and the floors were dirt. One man remarked on the horrible conditions, noting that the wounded "were ranged along on blankets, stretched on the bare earth. They lay in their ordinary clothing, in many instances stiff with blood. . . . Some were delirious and groaning with pain, some dying, some dead."[1]

In addition to their crude surroundings, the injured men also suffered from the fact that even the most accomplished of doctors, practicing in the finest hospitals of New York or Philadelphia, had little real understanding of how germs spread. Consequently, they made no effort even to wash their surgical instruments or their hands between patients, and sterilization was completely unknown. They saw a lot of their surgical patients die of infection after apparently successful operations, but they had not yet connected the onset of infection with the lack of cleanliness of the wound. And since fevers and other sicknesses were practically endemic, even among the soldiers who came through the battles unscathed, doctors often spread disease from one wounded man to another through their unsanitary surgical practices.

From Jalapa, General Scott quickly sent General Worth's division on ahead to occupy Perote, the next major town on the road to Mexico City. Upon arrival, Worth's troops found and freed some American prisoners of war being held in Fort San Carlos, the same fort which had served as the prison for some of the Texian prisoners captured at Santa Fe and at Mier a few years earlier.

Jalapa, Mexico
April 26th 1847

My dear Father

I find myself on the eve of departure for Perote, having made a stay of four days in this beautiful place, or rather it has been four days since we first arrived and have been so busy that I have not had time to write to you before.

Our Army pursued the fleeing enemy, and we came along as soon as we could collect our train and two days march brought us to this place.

The enemy out ran us and we failed to take many more prisoners. When the advance neared this place it was met by a deputation from the city asking that we would not molest them offering us the city.

Genl Worth pursued on, but the enemy passed by their strong holds, many spiking the guns to prevent our using them. At Perote, a very strongly fortified place, an officer met Genl Worth with an invoice of the stores to be turned over, and he marched into and took possession of the place.

As soon as I arrived here, I was sent back to the battle ground to send off some cannon as trophies for the United States. I sent off six pieces, four of them of Mexican manufacture, one named "El Terror del Norte Americano." As soon as Gen Scott heard that there had been taken such a piece, with such a name, he immediately determined that it should be sent to the United States and I was sent down to expedite the business. This occupied me nearly three days and since I have been back I have been very busy in one thing or other breaking up the arms we found here and preparing to leave.

The country in this vicinity is the most beautiful I have ever seen, growing more beautiful as one approached the place.

The climate is delightful, not too warm or too cold but a pleasant medium, as pleasant a climate or more so than I ever felt before.

We find here a great variety of fruits here oranges, bananas, plantains, pine apples &c. and it is quite a treat to get some fine fruit. I wish you could participate with me in some of the fine oranges we have here. For the first time I have seen some respectable decent looking people, since I have been in Mexico. Here you may see as well dressed people as anywhere. They are particularly noticable for the extreme whiteness and neatness of their linen and the good taste of their dress. Very few of the individuals have left, but seem to be pursuing their daily avocations the same as usual. All seem to be busy and flourishing from the presence of our Army.

Yesterday was Sunday and I went to the Cathedral to see if I could understand any part of the service. It surpassed anything I ever saw very different indeed. It is very richly ornamented, a great deal of gilt work, pictures, and wax images dressed up with a great deal of tinsel. The Church is paved, as are all of the houses, with a square brick made for the purpose, has no seats, the worshippers kneeling or standing during the whole of the service. Those that I saw there seemed to be mostly of the lower class, very few of the higher class.

I had no manual of their devotions and I could not distinguish what was said, and was not edified. Theirs is a religion that addresses itself to the senses and I think one could hardly enter without feeling reverently. This was the second time that I ever was present at their service, and I could so little understand what was going on that I have no desire to attend frequently. I wish I could unite with them or if I only had the opportunity of joining in the services of my own church I would be contented.

We hear that Genl Taylor is at San Louis Potosi which we hardly know whether to believe or not—we may meet him at Mexico, yet. We hear, now, that the Mexicans are not going to make peace at all, that if we go to Mexico they will change the place of the Capital and fight the guerrilla warfare. They are busy casting their bells into guns with no great success. We have taken from them a great number of cannon, at Perote some 54 of various calibres. There has been such talking all around me that I hardly know what I have written.

You have noticed my promotion, I suppose, to a first Lieutenancy. This gives me no increase of pay but is of importance to me when I am thrown with other officers.

Once more adieu.

My love to all. Your affectionate son

Theodore

⁘ • ⁘

The cannons that Laidley arranged to send back to the United States went to the Military Academy at West Point. They are among a total of ninety captured bronze cannons returned to his alma mater from Mexico. Five of them are 4-pounders, and the three with dates on them were all made in the early 1770s. The sixth gun, "El Terror del Norte Americano," was a brand new (1846) 8-pounder that now lies alongside other captured ordnance at Trophy Point, overlooking the Hudson River at West Point.[2]

This letter marks the first time that Laidley comments about the local populace, and his evaluation seems particularly positive.

He also seems to have a much more open mind than most of his contemporaries when it came to passing judgment upon the predominant religion in Mexico. He seems to have had a genuine interest in at least learning a little bit about the Catholic service.

This letter also mentions the rumor that General Taylor may be advancing southward from the Saltillo area, but of course this was not to be.

---

[1] Louis C. Duncan, "Medical History of General Scott's Campaign to the City of Mexico, 1847," *Military Surgeon* 47, no. 4 (1920), 454.

[2] Walter J. Nock, Museum Specialist, West Point Museum, to James M. McCaffrey, November 20, 1995.

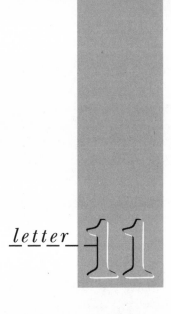

letter 11

As the American soldiers continued their unbroken string of military victories, they began to attribute some of their success to an inherent flaw in their opponents' personalities. Nothing else, after all, could reasonably account for the fact that they allowed the Americans to drive them out of one nearly impregnable position after another. After the fall of Veracruz and San Juan d'Ulúa, and the subsequent inspection of Mexican defenses by the victorious Americans, one artillery officer remarked that he could not "conceive of a place capable of a stronger defence," and that "all we saw increased our surprise at the surrender, with so many resources of war."[1]

Perote, Mexico May 3ʳᵈ 1847

My dear Father

You see I am at present in that city that has been rendered somewhat celebrated as the prison of the Santa Fe traders and others of our countrymen. It is distant 33 miles from Jalapa.

The road runs through a mountainous country presenting at times the most sublime prospects, and affording positions to the inhabitants where they might repel an overpowering foe. There is one pass between this and Jalapa that is regarded as stronger than that of Cerro Gordo. You will observe that in one of my former letters I spelled this last name differently; that was the English way, and this last the Mexican, as the Mexican has become fashionable I adopt it.

The Mexicans had begun to fortify this pass, but we came upon them so much sooner than they had any idea we would, they deserted them in their unfinished condition. A resolute band of men judiciously placed would [have], nevertheless, greatly impeded our progress and much diminished our ranks in passing those great strong holds of nature.

During the whole of our march till within a few miles of this place, we were continually ascending, and though we started with pleasant summer weather we were soon in the regions of spring and an overcoat was pleasant.

Perote is situated on a large plain, gently undulating, and the famous castle in stead of being perched up on some commanding eminence, as I, and as generally preconceived, is not a castle at all but a very regularly built, complete fort, built on the broad plains in front of the city. The fort surpasses anything we can boast in the U.S. in the way of completeness of its several parts. It is nearly as large as Fort Monroe, constructed in the same manner.

It is surrounded by a deep and wide ditch, and from the bottom of ditch to the top of the wall is 33 ft of solid masonry. Its form is of this shape. [see sketch, p. 82] A regular bastioned work on a quadrilateral. Those little marks on the edge represent the guns it is intended to mount. They had taken many of them to the Cerro Gorde—leaving only thirty five mounted, several dismounted. A [labeled in sketch] represent the Quarters for men and officers built very substantially of stone, 2 stories high and capable of accomodating 2,000 men. Genl Worth marched in his whole division of 2500 men and in time of a siege it might be made to contain many more. Opposite the Quarters across a wide street or alley are the workshops, store rooms, Magazines, Stables, &c &c all complete. It is their grand Arsenal where they put up most of their ammunitions, and a large amount of stores of all Kinds tools etc. we found stored up for use. The length of the line I have above traced is nearly a mile, outside of that is the broad and deep ditch, both sides laid in solid masonry, and outside of this are strong pickets and other defences. So upon the whole it is a <u>very strong</u> place and would have puzzled us mightily to have taken it, if they had not run off and left it. The city of Perote is no city at all, but rather an old village, an appendage to the fort. There are barracks and a few good buildings in it, the rest are poor things, going to ruin. The few, of the higher, class deserted their houses on our approach and I am now writing from one of their apartments. The houses very unfinished and scarcely any furniture at all. It is built on the side of a square the rooms opening out in the square where there is a fountain of fresh water and many flower pots of various flowers. The house is built one story high, flat roof, and the watch dog paces the roof and gives timely notice of any suspicious looking characters.

The rooms are more or less damp, being stone in all directions, and no fire places for building a fire.

The weather is that of spring, cold nights, and warm sun—it rains every afternoon, and the top of a neighboring hill, the other morning was capped with snow. There is a mountain some thirty miles from here which we have seen from Vera Cruz all along till this place whose summit is covered with perpetual snow.[2] It looked strange enough from the burning sands of the coast, and many were inclined to doubt the testimony of their own eyes, but coming up the country and finding the weather growing colder and colder it does not seem strange but all a matter of course. In a clear atmosphere it may be seen at a very great distance—being frequently seen by ships many miles from the shore.

Yesterday was Sunday and you will hardly believe me when I tell you I went to church and heard the service of my own church. It was an agreeable surprise to me to learn that there was a chaplain with the Army one from New York under the late act of Congress. It was a great pleasure once more to hear and enter in the familiar services as laid down in our prayer book and heartily I enjoyed. I hope it may not now be the last time I may have the opportunity. As long as I am with Gen Worth's division I may enjoy it, and we shall most likely be with him till we reach Puebla.

For this last place we expect to march in a few days, and after this I expect our communications with Vera Cruz will be pretty nearly cut off, so do not be surprised if you should not hear of the Army during the summer.

Santa Anna is on our flank and will endeavor to cut off our communications, and the extreme sickliness of the season will prevent our sending down to Vera Cruz, but we will endeavor to subsist on the country that we pass through.

I do not see that we are a bit nearer a peace now than when we first started—we have had victory after victory and seem to gain nothing by it. Will we be any nearer when we have taken the city of Mexico? I rather doubt it.

A Mexican officer gave himself up, the other day, to Gen Worth desiring to be sent to the U.S. saying he was tired of seeing his countrymen so cut to pieces on all sides. Would that they all were as sensible!

You recollect that all letters to the Army come free, now, why not deluge me with them? A mail comes at long intervals, still they come and come without anything for me. It is not pleasant. Stir up there, cold friends.

With much love, your affectionate son

<u>Theodore</u>

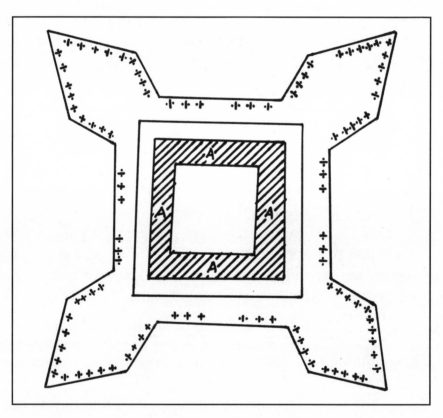

From Laidley's sketch of the fort at Perote

❖ • ❖

Laidley again alludes in this letter to what he and most other American observers perceived as a tremendous lack of patriotism on the part of the Mexican soldiers.

Laidley's description of the fort at Perote is quite extensive, as one might expect from such a carefully schooled officer. Other contemporary observations mention that the names of many of the Texian prisoners once held there could still be seen scratched into the walls of the cells. When American soldiers saw such evidences of what they believed to be Mexican cruelty, it seemed to make them all the more anxious to meet and defeat Santa Anna's force once and for all.

The appearance with the army of Reverend John McCarty and other Protestant chaplains gave a boost to men such as Lieutenant Laidley, although many other soldiers still failed to observe the Sabbath with any regularity. McCarty had spent about a year as a U.S. Navy chaplain in the mid 1820s, and had then returned to civilian life. Then on February 11, 1847, Congress authorized ten new regiments of regular troops for service against Mexico, and the same bill also allowed for the appointment of brigade chaplains. McCarty joined the army two months later, but this time he stayed in the military service for twenty more years.[3]

---

[1] William Austine to his brother, April 1, 1847, in "America's First D-Day: The Veracruz Landing of 1847," ed. James M. McCaffrey, *Military History of the West* 25, no. 1 (Spring 1995), 66.

[2] This peak is known as Orizaba.

[3] "An act to raise for a limited time an additional military force, and for other purposes," in *The Military Laws of the United States Relating to the Army, Volunteers, Militia, and to Bounty Lands and Pensions from the Foundation of the Government to the Year 1863*, ed. John F. Callan (Philadelphia: George W. Childs, 1863), 379–80; Francis Bernard Heitman, *Historical Register and Dictionary of the United States Army, from Its Organization, September 29, 1789, to March 2, 1903* (Washington, D.C.: Government Printing Office, 1903), vol. 2, 654.

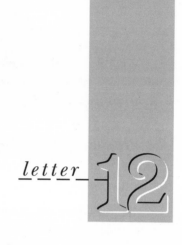

On May 10, General Worth's division headed out of Perote for Puebla, some ninety miles away. By the 14th, most of his men had reached Amozoc, about ten miles short of their goal. There had been increased guerrilla activity in the neighborhood, however, so Worth decided to wait there for the arrival of his more slowly moving pack trains under Major General John A. Quitman. It was fortunate that the main body waited, because Santa Anna had sent some of his cavalry to attack Quitman's train. When the horsemen saw that Worth had sent reinforcments to Quitman they called off their attack and once again retreated toward Mexico City. The next morning Worth's 4,200-man force entered the city of Puebla, a city of 80,000 inhabitants. Here it would await the arrival of the rest of the army.

In the meantime, President Polk, encouraged by the outcome of the siege of Veracruz, decided to sent a diplomat to Scott's army to be on hand to carry out the inevitable peace plan. The idea made sense. In those days of slow communications and even slower travel, a considerable amount of time would have elapsed between the time the Mexican government agreed to talks and the time it would take for the news to reach

Washington and a suitable representative of the government dispatched. Polk's plan meant that as soon as the Mexicans hinted that they might be willing to negotiate an end to the war, a state department official would be right there on the scene to get the ball rolling.

The choice for this delicate position was Nicholas P. Trist, the bilingual, experienced Chief Clerk of the State Department. On April 15, Trist received the various necessary documents for his trip, which included his formal commission, the official announcement to the Mexican foreign minister of his purpose with Scott's army, and a draft copy of a proposed treaty of peace. The treaty called for establishing the boundary of Texas at the Rio Grande River, the U.S. acquisition of New Mexico and California (both Alta California and Baja California), and the right of transit across the Isthmus of Tehuantepec. Polk further authorized Trist to offer up to thirty million dollars to effect these conditions, and he left Washington the next day.

Trist arrived at Veracruz on May 6, and immediately forwarded to General Scott his introduction to the Mexican foreign minister as well as instructions to Scott from the secretary of war regarding Trist's mission. Scott misinterpreted his instructions. He mistakenly believed that Trist was being placed in a position from which to dictate to the army, and told Trist that he would not defer to him in what he considered purely military matters unless Trist was "clothed with military rank over me."[1]

When Trist wrote to Scott, the general petulantly refused even to open the letters until days, or weeks, after he had received them. When he did read them he took offense at their tone and told Trist, "If you dare to use the style of orders or instructions again, or indulge yourself in a single discourteous phrase, I shall throw back the communication with the contempt & scorn which you merit at my hands."[2]

What President Polk had intended to be a time saving measure had rapidly deteriorated into something vastly different. It would be impossible for Trist to work out a negotiated settlement of the war if Scott would not only refuse to forward Trist's letter to the Mexican foreign secretary but even refused to speak to him.

Puebla, Mexico May 19th 1847

My dear Father

It is said there will be a chance of sending to the states tomorrow, and not wishing that any opportunity should escape of letting you hear from me, I write at any rate; however, thinking it very probable that his Excellency Genl Santa Anna may have the first reading and perhaps deprive you, entirely, of hearing of my safe arrival at this City.

We heard of the enemy in our advance and fully expected an attack in passing a famous pass in the mountains between Perote and this place, but we were disappointed—it seems they contemplated making a stand but afterwards gave it up. About 10 miles from here we called a halt preparatory to marching into this place, were very quiet not supposing that an enemy was anywhere near when upon a sudden we were called to arms, Mexicans being in sight. The troops were called out, and sent to make an attack, but the enemy consisting of 3,000 cavalry kept well out of the way and our artillery did but little execution.

Not having but a very small squadron of cavalry they got out of our way. They not firing a single shot—we took several prisoners and killed some twenty.

After having passed us and well gotten out of sight they made a circuitous route and returned to this place. What was their object we have not satisfactorily learned: some say to attack [Maj.] Genl [John A.] Quitman who was advancing to overtake us, and who had not over a thousand volunteers, and others say to prevent our march directly on this place to cover the withdrawal of stores from this place on towards Mexico.

We marched into this City on Sat. 13th inst. and it was a grand holiday for the citizens who lined the streets on either side wherever we went on our way to the main plaza.

The city is said to contain 75,000 inhabitants and is as pretty a city as I ever saw situated in the middle of a valley by far the most lovely that I ever beheld.

I am placed at Fort Loretto on a hill commanding the city and have a grand view of the whole city, the vast valley, the famous pyramid of Cholula in the distance and still farther in the distance the two mountains Popocatapetl and another with such a hard name [Iztaccihuatl] that I will not attempt to write it, and I know you would not pronounce it if I did, whose summits are continually clad with snow.

It is a view of singular beauty and magnificence the like whereof I have never seen before.

There is a very great number of churches and many of great architectural pretensions.

The Cathedral is very large and very elegant, I hear for I have not been able to see it as yet, as in fact I have not been any where owing to a violent cold that I have had since I have been here. The sun is so extremely hot and the rooms damp from their thick walls that many of us are suffering from colds. I hope to see the city throughout before we leave it as well as make a visit to the pyramid.

We hear that General Santa Anna is in advance preparing to check our advance any further into the interior but if he makes no more than he did at Cerro Gordo, he might as well give up. There is no hope for peace as yet, and the foreigners here think that we will have to call in such a force as to overun the country entirely before they will think of coming to terms. Strange stubbornness on their part!

They will get whipped so soundly the next time that they will begin to open their eyes. All of the paroled prisoners have been compelled to take up arms again by their Generals, the probability is that so so[me] will not be taken.

The higher classes receive us as kindly as they dare, the lower classes, those whom we are doing great service are our bitterest foes, through ignorance with which their generals keep them slaves and with regard to us—They think us little better than devils and are ready to cut our throats the first opportunity that offers.

General Scott is expected up in a day or so, when we hope to get a mail with some news from the states and some letters I hope from you.

Give my love to the family

Yours very affectionately
Theodore

Laidley realizes that communications between the American army in the interior of Mexico and the occupation troops at Veracruz—and by extension with the United States—was constantly hampered by the large numbers of Mexican bandits and irregular troops that waited to ambush individual couriers as well as fairly large supply trains. Obviously, since this letter did reach its destination, some of the mail made it through. Some soldiers numbered their letters home. That way, if some of their letters wound up in the hands of robbers their correspondent would note a gap in the numbering sequence and be able to inform the soldier so he could rewrite that particular letter and send it again. Likewise, the folks at home sometimes used this same method of tracking their correspondence.

Laidley finally begins to draw contrasts among the different social classes of Mexican civilians he encounters, a practice that was quite common among the American soldiers. The occupying soldiers usually ascribed higher morals to those Mexicans they saw with lighter skins, believing that they must be Spaniards instead of Mexicans. An Alabama volunteer officer confided to his diary that he had seen a wide variation of color at a recent fandango. "The copper coloured Mexican, the dark skinned & the red indian-like natives were here," he wrote, as were a few "fair complexioned Castillians." An Ohio officer also drew distinctions among the "haughty Castillians in whose veins flowed the pure blood of Cortes, the yellow aztec, the stupid Indian and the decrepid negro."[3]

---

[1] K. Jack Bauer, *The Mexican War* (New York: Macmillan, 1974), 283.

[2] Bauer, 283.

[3] Sydenham Moore diary, January 19?, 1847, Alabama State Archives, Montgomery, Alabama; John W. Lowe to his wife, October 10, 1847, John Williamson Lowe letters, Dayton and Montgomery County Public Library, Dayton, Ohio.

By the end of May, General Scott had once again consoli-
dated his force, but a problem arose that made it impossible for
him to go onward. The war was now slightly over a year old, and
the twelve-month enlistments of the volunteers were beginning
to expire. Whatever discipline problems these amateur soldiers
presented, they fought like veterans and constituted a considerable percentage of Scott's force. If he could not persuade them
to reenlist, or to extend their present enlistments for a few
months, he would not have enough troops to wage offensive
warfare.

Efforts to induce the volunteers to stay past their originally
scheduled dates of departure were universally unsuccessful. The
overwhelming response to the plea to reenlist for the war was,
in effect, no thanks! The thinking seemed to be that they had
made a contract with the government. The arrangement was
that in exchange for a certain specified salary plus food they
would agree to be soldiers. But the agreement had a one-year
time limit on it. Now that the year was almost over, so was the
agreement. The men had no qualms about leaving the army in
the situation that prevailed. They had left home with visions of

earning battlefield glory for themselves, but after a year of service most were willing to admit that there was very little of glory to be had, and that was hard earned. Instead they had seen their friends waste away and die of disease, not gallantly leading charges against the enemy. No, if there was still glory to be won, they seemed to suggest, let someone else have a chance at winning it. They, after all, had carried out their part of the bargain, and now they were ready to return to their homes and loved ones. If the government still needed more soldiers, let it make deals with a fresh set of men.

The commanding general appealed to their patriotism, asking them to stay with the army for the duration of the war. The men of the Alabama volunteer regiment made a counteroffer when it came time to consider reenlisting. They agreed to do so, but only for a period of three months. If, at the end of that time, the American forces were not completely victorious they would go home anyway and let others see the war to its conclusion. Scott, of course, could not allow the volunteers to dictate the terms of their service and declined the offer.[1]

Luckily, Congress had passed legislation on February 11, 1847, authorizing the formation of ten more regular regiments—nine of infantry and one of dragoons. In addition, the secretary of war now issued calls to various state governors to supply more volunteer regiments. In some cases these were additional requirements, but for many states in the east it was their first call for troops. None of the new soldiers were allowed to sign up for only twelve months. Their terms of enlistment were for five years or for the duration of the war.

❖ • ❖

Puebla, Mexico, June 3ᵈ 1847

My dear Father

The occasion of breaking up the post at Jalapa and sending down to withdraw the troops and stores from that place presents a favorable opportunity of sending down a letter that far, trusting that it may reach you before long.

Since my last from this place Genl Scott with the rest of the troops has arrived and we are now patiently waiting for reinforcements, at the same time the motives of the Mexican Government. We are glad of the Genl's arrival for Gen Worth had the troops under arms the greater portion of the time constantly expecting an attack, and several times had it reported and believed or seemed to believe, that the enemy, in large numbers, was close on us ready to attack us.

He is famous for getting up <u>stampedes</u> and [inspires] a want of confidence that a General should not, a constant fear of attack which harasses himself and his troops.

I have had but little to do since my arrival at this place, a good deal of leisure time to devote to such purposes as pleased me. I have read a little, and gone around the [town] and visited portions of the city worthy of notice, and am more pleased with its appearance the more I see of it.

The famous Cathedral received a share of my attention and it is altogether a new thing to me in the way of architecture. It is very large indeed and the interior is one blaze of gilt, and pictures, some of them very fine. The altar is the most magnificent of anything I have seen—numerous beautiful statues, sacred subjects, are placed around and over it, and though not so splendid as it has been, still it is, now, to us who, in the States, are not accustomed to such things, something new and very striking. There is service every day from early in the day till one o'clock and then again in the evening. At whatever time you go there you find persons engaged in worship, a great number do not eat till they have been to mass.

There are numerous churches besides, some of them very beautiful, but not worthy of description when compared with the Cathedral. The number of priests is very great, they are to be seen in every direction at all times, and are not at all times those exemplary persons that their calling requires of them.

There are several large public squares in the place that constitute an important feature in the beauty of the place. They abound in trees, shrubs, plants and flowers of every description with fountains interspersed here and there, forming altogether a most beautiful promenade and ride, for which purposes it is very much resorted to in the cool of the evening—but bands of music play almost every evening which renders it additionally agreeable. There are several points near the city from which the most beautiful prospects are visible, embracing a field of vast extent and singular magnificence.

I am very much pleased with the climate and the country, and only regret that the hostile feeling of the people prevents our seeing more of it, and moving more at our own pleasure than we can at present do.

This is a great day among the Mexicans called Corpus Christi or body of Christ. This morning there was a great of ringing of bells, even more than usual and I understand they formed processions and marched about through the church with numerous lighted wax candles, and gave them to many of our officers to carry, whom curiosity had taken there. It is customary I understand, to carry what they call the body of Christ around through the streets, forming a grand procession, but owing to the presence of our army or as they express it to such a number of heretics, they confine their processions and great doing to the churches.

This evening the bull fight comes off and most of the officers are absent to see it. There is a large place permanently fitted for this exhibition, though this is the first since our arrival. This is always the way with this people the latter part of their holy days, every Sunday, is spent at some place of amusement, a bull fight, fandango, or something of the kind.

There are many circumstances under which they seem to us very singular, and many in which they are very far behind the civilized world.

Their agriculture is of the ancient[?] kind. I saw some ploughing the other day by a pair of oxen, the plough made of rough wood not of the approved shape with a little iron point—it made a small furrow and a man followed, dropped the corn and covered it with his feet keeping up with the slow pace of the oxen. Here is the fellow's plough: [see sketch, p. 95] Would you like to secure one like it? The end of the pole is fastened to the yoke which is in turn fastened to the horns, instead [of] pulling from the shoulder they pull by their heads.

We are not expecting to march till the troops come up from Jalapa, perhaps not then as it is believed we will "conquer a peace" sooner by remaining here than by pushing on to the city of Mexico.

We can go there if we thought it would do[?] but, of this there are serious doubts—Santa Anna having resigned there is some hopes a peace man may be elected, and who may be disposed to treat of this I have but little hopes.[2] I cannot see how it is ever going to terminate. Mr. [Nicholas] Trist the commissioner is here with the army but the Gen declines being ordered by him to do anything, says he will obey the orders of anyone who bears the commission of Lieutenant General, but of no citizen.

I received your letters of March 20th and 27th in safety. I am thankful that your fears proved not true and pray that I may be preserved in safety from the many dangers to which I am exposed. It is an act of mercy that I have been preserved thus far.

My health is better. I still have those disagreeable symptoms that I have been troubled with but I am looking better and am fleshier than I was when I left.[3] The more actively employed I am the better I am.

We had morning service last Sunday and shall have I suppose as long as we remain here—this is my greatest consolation. The mail sometimes brings me a religious paper or a letter from you which stirs me up and brings to mind more vividly my duties to my God and I start again with renewed resolution of constancy and fidelity to my God.

Give my love to all.

Your affectionate son
<u>Theodore</u>

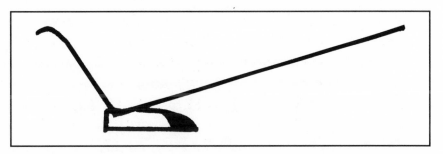

From Laidley's sketch of a plow

❧ • ❧

Laidley, like most American soldiers who commented upon
Mexican churches, was awed by their material splendor. Several
men wrote descriptions of the seventeenth-century cathedral at
Puebla in their letters home describing the massive marble col-
umns and the rich silver and gold candlesticks. Many repeated
the local legend of supernatural help while it was being built.
The story was that at the end of each work day, after the work-
men had gone home, angels came down and continued construction. Then, each morning the returning workers would be
astounded to see that the angels had accomplished as much
overnight as they had during the previous day.[4]

Laidley's evaluation of the clergy as being less than exemplary at all times is mild compared to the judgments some of
his fellow soldiers offered. One soldier described how Sunday,
the day of worship, was also a day of much celebration in Mexican towns. This was the day that bullfights occurred, that cock-
fights were staged, and that much drinking and carousing went
on. Indeed, one Sunday in Saltillo he attended a cockfight and
noticed that one of the most active bettors—and winners—was
the local priest. One of Laidley's classmates at West Point, South
Carolinian Daniel H. Hill, confided to his diary that "the bloated
and sensual appearance of the [local] priest was disgusting and
revolting. He has two daughters in town and 'tis a matter of
common notoriety."[5]

The majority of U.S. soldiers were Protestants and had very
little knowledge of Catholic ceremony. When they witnessed it
among the people of Mexico they often made light of it. In one
instance, some Ohio volunteers observed a priest in Puebla
making the sign of the cross with ashes on the foreheads of the
faithful on Ash Wednesday. One of their officers remarked that
this was "the most foolish thing I ever saw." So comical did these

soldiers find the proceedings that they soon carved a cross from a piece of cork and "marked each other all over their faces until the Mexicans felt ashamed and wiped theirs off."[6]

Even though it was the strict policy of the U.S. Army to respect the religious practices of the local people, many soldiers found that to be very difficult in spite of attempts to be as understanding as possible. In nearby Jalapa, Colonel Thomas Childs decided that he and three of his officers would actually take part in one of the local religious processions through town as a sort of goodwill gesture. At the appointed time the officers, with caps in one hand and lighted candles in the other, left the church with the other celebrants. This gesture, in itself, might not have generated more than passing comment from the less religiously inclined rank and file. But the colonel had given orders ahead of time that American soldiers on sentry duty along the line of march were to present arms upon the approach of the procession. Then, grasping their muskets in their left hands, they were to remove their caps with their rights and kneel until the host had passed. This left a bad taste in the mouths of many of the volunteers on duty that day, and most of them refused to abide by this request. One man, in fact, thought the whole thing to be not only absurd but probably unconstitutional as well. It may be that when word of this incident reached Puebla that church officials there decided to do away with the public processions and keep that particular ceremony within the walls of the church.[7]

Lieutenant Laidley continued to be consoled by the religious services that Reverend McCarty offered. On this particular Sunday his text was "I would not live always," which seemed particularly appropriate for an army at war. Although battle with the enemy was not contributing any deaths at Puebla at this time to lend poignancy to the topic, men were dying of disease daily. This could not have been lost on Laidley at the time.[8]

[1] S. F. Nunnelee, "Alabama in Mexico War," *Alabama Historical Quarterly* 19 (1957), 430.

[2] Santa Anna offered his resignation as President of Mexico on May 28, 1847, but when the congress seemed on the verge of accepting it he withdrew the offer. John Edward Weems, *To Conquer a Peace: The War Between the United States and Mexico* (Garden City, New York: Doubleday, 1974), 386–87.

[3] Whatever troubling symptoms Laidley had are still a mystery.

[4] Frances Calderon de la Barca, *Life in Mexico* (1843; reprint, New York: Dutton, 1970), 337–38.

[5] T. H. Towner to his father, July 27, 1847, Benjamin Towner papers, Duke University Library, Durham, North Carolina; Daniel Harvey Hill diary, September 6, 1846, University of North Carolina Library, Chapel Hill, North Carolina.

[6] John W. Lowe to Pinckney Fishback, March 9, 1848, John Williamson Lowe letters, Dayton and Montgomery County Library, Dayton, Ohio.

[7] George Ballentine, *Autobiography of an English Soldier in the United States Army* (1853, reprint, Chicago: R. R. Donnelly and Sons, 1986), 227–29.

[8] Ralph W. Kirkham, *The Mexican War Journal and Letters of Ralph W. Kirkham*, ed. Robert Ryal Miller (College Station: Texas A&M University Press, 1991), 19–20.

By early June, General Scott faced a real problem within his army. The seven volunteer regiments whose terms of enlistment had expired were on their way home, leaving him in the middle of a hostile country with an army of barely seven thousand men.[1] The general now set about consolidating his command at Puebla to await the arrival of reinforcements from the United States. Luckily, the Mexican political situation was in such a state of flux that Santa Anna was unable to gather together enough troops to destroy the small force of foreign invaders. Until the additional troops arrived from the United States, the soldiers at Puebla spent their time on garrison details, with an occasional raid against some nearby Mexican bandit band.

Relations between General Scott and Nicholas Trist began to thaw during the summer. Scott finally realized that the State Department agent was there to work in concert with him and not to undermine him in any way. The general then broke the ice in early July when, after Trist had come down sick, Scott sent him a box of guava marmalade to enjoy during his recovery. Within a week the two men had become fast friends and were working together harmoniously.

By the end of the first week in August, approximately 4,500 replacements had reached Puebla, and General Scott finalized plans to move against Mexico City. His army now totaled almost 15,000 men, although the newcomers were untested in battle and almost 4,000 of his veteran troops were ill and unable to march. He designated Brevet Colonel Thomas Childs to remain behind with the convalescents and a small garrison in Puebla while the rest of the army pushed on. Among Colonel Childs's staff officers was Lieutenant Laidley.

The vanguard of Scott's army reached the town of Ayotla on August 11 and stopped. From here the Mexican capital was just a day's march west, but there were several possible routes. After careful reconnaissance by Captain Robert E. Lee, Lieutenant George B. McClellan, and others, General Scott chose the southernmost route into the city and issued orders on August 15 to begin the final approach.

On August 19, American and Mexican soldiers tangled near Contreras, southwest of the capital. The Mexican commander, Major General Gabriel Valencia, brushed off reports that the Americans had made their way successfully through an ancient lava bed and would soon be in a position to defeat him. The petrified refuse of some ancient volcano could be traversed by a man on foot, but its craggy folds would certainly not allow the passage of a body of troops with their wagons and artillery. Unfortunately for Valencia, the rumors proved all too true, and the fighting the next day resulted in another in the unbroken string of American military victories. With a loss of only about sixty men killed and wounded, the Americans killed seven hundred enemy soldiers and captured even more than that. Just as important as the prisoners, however, was the fact that the Mexicans also gave up twenty-two pieces of artillery and huge numbers of small arms and ammunition.[2]

Later on the same day, another battle took place on the east side of the lava bed, culminating in an American victory at Churubusco. This time, however, the victory was not so one-sided. The Mexicans put up a valiant defense, and even though Santa Anna lost another two thousand men in killed and wounded, Scott's butcher bill was also very high. He lost twelve percent of his 8,500-man force, including 133 killed.[3]

General Scott and Nicholas Trist both hoped that the twin American victories at Contreras and Churubusco would surely convince Mexican authorities to begin serious peace negotiations. In fact, developments in that direction were forthcoming on the very next day. A Mexican officer entered American lines under a flag of truce and related to General Scott Santa Anna's verbally expressed wishes for an armistice during which negotiators would seek a permanent halt in the fighting. Scott was willing to give it a try, citing the great loss of life already suffered in what he termed an "unnatural war between the two great Republics" on the North American continent.[4]

Both sides agreed to a formal armistice on August 23. Under its terms neither army could receive reinforcements or strengthen its military position while negotiations went on. Prisoners of war would be released, and American quartermasters would be allowed to enter Mexico City to purchase food supplies for the temporarily idle American army outside its gates.

Formal efforts to turn the armistice into a lasting peace began when Trist met with Mexican authorities in the town of Atzcapuzalco on August 27. Initial Mexican demands were entirely out of line with what Trist had been ordered to seek. For example, even though the Mexicans now seemed willing to acknowledge the loss of Texas they were still not ready to accept the Rio Grande as its border but wanted it to be at the Nueces. They would not willingly give up California but were willing only to negotiate its ownership, and only that part north of 26°

north latitude. American troops would have to remain outside of Mexico City, and they would have to return all captured cannons and other trophies of war. Trist must have scratched his head and wondered if the Mexicans believed that they were *winning* the war and not losing it.

By September 1, the Mexican peace commissioners had relaxed their demands a little, but they still demanded the Nueces boundary and the retention of New Mexico. California was still subject to negotiation. The two sides were still too far apart for any meaningful compromise to be possible. On September 3, Santa Anna showed his true character by cutting off further food sales to the Americans. He also had been using the time to strengthen his position, in direct violation of the terms of the armistice, so on September 6, General Scott announced that the armistice would end in forty-eight hours.

On the evening of September 7, Scott received a report that the Mexicans were using some mill buildings southwest of the city to melt down heavy bronze church bells and cast them into cannons. Although the report later proved inaccurate, the general decided on an immediate attack. General William J. Worth's division, slightly over three thousand men, would carry out the assault at dawn the next day. The resulting fight—the Battle of Molino del Rey—was probably the most vicious and costly of any of Scott's battles.

Inadequate reconnaissance led General Worth to believe that the Mexicans had all but abandoned the stone buildings that were his target. He therefore sent his infantry forward with only a slight artillery preparation. Far from having abandoned the buildings, the Mexicans were there in force, and when they opened their artillery on the advancing formations of American infantry the effects were devastating. In several sections of the field, Americans were seen to fall back temporarily, regroup, and then move forward again into the deadly fire. Finally, after

two hours, American counterbattery fire proved to be too effective for continued resistance, and the Mexicans began a slow
withdrawal from the buildings. By this time the American infantry had reached the buildings and was engaged in bitter
room-to-room fighting. When it was all over, the Battle of Molino
del Rey went into the record books as another American victory, but one that had been very costly. Altogether, Worth's division suffered approximately twenty-five percent casualties, and
the end of the war seemed to be no nearer than before.[5]

On September 11, General Scott called his top subordinates
together for a council of war. It was time to decide how best to
proceed against the defenses of Mexico City itself. Although
there was not a consensus—some favored attacking from the
south and others from the west—Scott opted for the latter approach. First, however, it would be necessary to reduce the cita-
del of Chapultepec, just southwest of the capital and adjacent
to Molino del Rey.

Scott of course wanted to keep Santa Anna from discerning
his plans, so while his engineer officers selected sites from which
to bombard Chapultepec he had other troops demonstrating
in the direction of the southern approaches to the city. And the
ruse worked. Santa Anna was forced to keep his troops dispersed
to cover several possible approaches to the city and was unable
to respond with reinforcements when the American guns
opened on Chapultepec on September 12.

Bombardment by itself was not enough to force evacuation,
so Scott ordered an assault for the 13th. Again the cannons
opened up at dawn, and the attack began about 8 A.M. There
were problems; the troops who were to scale the walls of the
castle arrived before their scaling ladders did, for example. But
eventually the pressure once more proved overwhelming and
what was left of the Mexican garrison surrendered at about 9:30.

The surrender of Chapultepec left the way open for an advance on Mexico City itself, and troops of Worth's and Quitman's divisions moved forward. Although they had defeated Chapultepec's defenders in only a few hours, it would take them the rest of the day to reach the gates of the city. Mexican resistance was fierce. It was here that three more of Lieutenant Laidley's classmates fell. Calvin Benjamin was killed and Mansfield Lovell and Earl Van Dorn were wounded.

Fighting stopped when darkness fell, and the exhausted men of both armies tried to get what rest they could before resuming hostilities the next day. During the night, however, Santa Anna decided to withdraw to the north and let the Americans have the city. On the morning of September 14, 1847, General Winfield Scott triumphantly entered the enemy capital, thus completing his epic campaign from Veracruz to Mexico City. The fall of the Mexican capital did not, however, signal an automatic end to the fighting. Santa Anna may have given up hopes of defending Mexico City, but he was certainly not ready to admit complete defeat. Instead he led a large force eastward toward the American garrison at Puebla. After all, if he could wipe out the relatively small garrison there he would effectively sever communication between General Scott and the United States, leading, perhaps, to the ultimate surrender of the American invaders.

Colonel Childs was certainly aware of his tenuous situation at Puebla. His force, in the middle of a city whose population approached 100,000, numbered only about 2,200. And only about 400 of these were healthy enough to take part in active campaigning. He consequently chose not to disperse his men over too wide an area. He stationed six companies, approximately 250 men, near his headquarters at the Cuartel de San José. From here they could also defend the large numbers of sick and wounded in the Cathedral de San José, which the

Americans had converted into a hospital. It was here, too, that Childs stationed Lieutenant Laidley to command a makeshift artillery contingent of one 12-pounder gun, one mountain howitzer, and four rocket batteries.

The remainder of the American garrison dug in on two hills on the northeastern outskirts of the city. They were close enough to Childs' headquarters to lend support if the enemy pressed an attack in that direction, and they could likewise depend upon reinforcements from the Cuartel de San José if necessary. A makeshift unit of walking wounded and other convalescents and a company of Pennsylvania volunteers defended Fort Loretto with the help of two 12-pounder guns and one ten-inch mortar. Slightly to the southeast another volunteer company from the Keystone State guarded Guadalupe Heights.[6]

On September 14, the very night that Santa Anna evacuated Mexico City, General Joaquín Rea's guerrillas staged a massive infiltration into Puebla. This was not difficult in light of the small force there to oppose it and the active help, or at least connivance, of a large part of the civilian population. Rea's men barricaded streets near the plaza of San José and effectively sealed off the main body of American troops from the detached units. By the time Colonel Childs was aware of their presence in the city, it was too late for him to consolidate his command. Those at Fort Loretto and on Guadalupe Heights would have to do the best they could.

General Rea, of course, knew from local informants and direct observation the scattered condition of the American garrison, and on September 16 he confidently called on Childs to surrender. When the American refused, some 500 Mexican horsemen attacked San José only to be driven back by heavy volleys of musketry and Laidley's well served artillery. The defenders similarly repulsed another attack two days later, but on September 22, Santa Anna arrived from Mexico City with more troops. The next day, their numbers raised to an estimated 8,000 and their hopes undoubtedly buoyed by the arrival of their leader, Mexican troops attacked again but gave up when they met with no success.[7]

Unable to drive the Americans from the stout defenses of the stone buildings around the San José plaza, Santa Anna resorted to one of the oldest tactics of warfare—a siege. He would attempt to cut off the Americans' food and water supplies until they had no options other than starvation or surrender. Colonel Childs received another surrender demand on September 25, and again he refused to do so even as Mexican troops forced their way closer and closer to his headquarters.

Word of the plight of the Americans at Puebla reached Veracruz, and Brigadier General Joseph Lane was soon on his way with reinforcements to lift the siege. On September 30, Santa Anna left Rea at Puebla to continue operations there while he led a 5,000-man force to intercept the relief column. Childs took advantage of the reduction in the enemy force facing him and launched several small counterattacks that helped relieve enemy pressure and were a great boost to American morale. He also managed to get word to General Lane to be on the watch for Santa Anna. Lane took heed, and when he learned of the presence of a Mexican ambush was able to turn the tables on Santa Anna. A brisk fight at Huamantla on October 9 sent the Mexicans scurrying for Querétaro, and Lane's column continued on toward Puebla.

The ringing of church bells from Guadalupe Heights signaled the approach of Lane's column on October 12, and it was truly joyous news for Laidley and his fellow defenders who had drawn their last meat ration three days earlier.

❧ • ❧

Puebla, Mexico Oct. 16th 1847

My dear Father

I know how anxious you are to hear from me after all the battles that have been fought at Mexico, to be assured that I have escaped unhurt, I have therefore occupied my first leisure moments after the termination of our siege to raise a few letters from other officers and engage a courier to attempt to carry them to Vera Cruz. I fear very much lest he should not be successful, the guerrilla parties are so thick along the road that it is almost impossible to escape their vigilance. But I embrace eagerly any chance of success to relieve you from your doubts and anxiety.

Yes, praise the Lord for his goodness, He has preserved my unprofitable life from the many dangers that have surrounded me; and when so many of [my] brother officers have been swept away I am still the spared monument of his mercy. What an incentive it should be, through His assistance it shall be, to lead a more holy life in future! I trust it shall not be without its benefit to me, to teach [me] to live that I shall always be prepared whenever I may be called. I know you will all join me in praising His name for thus preserving me and watching over me in the hours of danger.

I have had no opportunity of telling you before that I was not with the army at Mexico. It was very unexpected to me that I would have to remain. I did not know it till a few hours before I was going to start—Genl Scott said that he knew that this place would be attacked and that an Ordinance Officer must be left behind as a part of the regular garrison. I was very much disappointed I assure you, but I felt that all would turn out for the best and after failing to exchange with some of my brother officers who were going with the army, I endeavored to be contented and not complain.

The event has proved that though not exposed to so many dangers, perhaps as I would have been had I gone on, I have had a more disagreeable and fatiguing time here. I do not know how the Ordinance officers were engaged at Mexico, and what were their duties, as we are entirely cut off from them and all we know about them comes from New Orleans, strange as it appears.

During our siege I have played a pretty important part, knowing more about artillery than any one left here I was entrusted with the management of that part of the artillery that was at the post where I was stationed and Governor did me the honor to say that it was well done, and another time that he wished he had two or three officers like me, this last of course, was told to a third person, not to me.

I was a good deal exposed on several occasions—once when I was firing, the enemy tried to drive us from our guns and the balls fell pretty thick around us, but did no injury—the artillery did more good than all the rest put together.

At one time they were coming up the street leading to our post, but gave way to a few discharges of one of my guns.

We have had a long & fatiguing time of it—for twenty eight days they were continually firing at us, the balls were whizzing through the air where ever you went. It required us to be constantly on the watch, many of us did not sleep, scarcely at all, during the night, sometimes nod a little lying beside our guns. For more than a month I did not have my clothes off to sleep. Of course, cut off from the city & from every body else we had to take soldier's fare, bread & meat which last article gave out before reinforcments arrived. However we would have held out much longer before we would surrender to Santa Anna's eight thousand, though we had only some six hundred at either of the three separate posts and many of them were convalescents not worth the third of a well man.

Our loss was very small considering the circumstances, about twenty killed and some forty wounded, far less than that of the enemy—his loss will never be truly known though it most probably quadrupled ours.

And in every respect they suffered more than we—their own soldiers robbed and plundered as well as our own—many citizens found themselves reduced from affluent circumstances to poverty in a night's time.

I endured the fatigues better than I expected, the loss of sleep and exposure. I have been pretty well through it, able at all times to perform what was required of me—to be sure I was worn out pretty well before it was ended, but I am recuperating. Heretofore, I have said but little about my health, for though enabled to perform what was at any time required of me I still felt unwell, the same as when I left you. The causes of my indisposition still exist, though their effects are not so severely felt in this fine, equable, climate.[8]

My health is at present better than it has been for a long time, and I trust that it may still continue to improve, if no unseen event prevents.

My life is not as active as I would wish. Even now, we dare not go far from our troops, there are so many all around us who only want an opportunity to get us out of sight to assassinate us.

If I were in Mexico [City] it would be somewhat different—my bounds would be wider. My orders are to repair there as soon as the Governor says he can spare me—I shall try him the first time any troops leave for that place, when that will be I know not and I am, by no means, assured that the Governor will say he can spare me—I am anxious that he should, for all of the Regular Army is there, and all of my friends—there is a chaplain, and I have some pious friends whose society I would like to enjoy.

Here I am pretty much alone, and keep pretty much to myself, though they all seem to regard me highly and treat me kindly.

Among both officers and soldiers here I have gained a high reputation, without my having acted with that view—I tried to do what was my duty and left the consequences with Him who disposes of all things.

For the praise of men I do not think I care very much—to be sure it is pleasant to hear their good opinion when we do not sacrifice any principle of duty for it. I expect the Governor will speak well of me in his despatches, for which I only care that it will please you to know that your son has done his duty faithfully, so as to gain the approbation of his commanding officer. I do not think I am very ambitious of any thing else.

My dear father, I am pleased to say to you that nearly all of your letters have reached me. The last mail brought me five and the one before four so I hope you will feel encouraged to continue. You do not know what a pleasure it is to hear from [you], how much they encourage me to continue in the faithful discharge of my duty, and urge me on to be more faithful.

The last I received was Aug. 20th—I hope every mail will bring me a half dozen. They are such a comfort to me that I thank my God for giving me so good a father, who helps me to do my duty and cheers me on when desponding. May he long, long continue him to me and the rest of his family! Yes, my father, I have good friends in New York, who next to yourself are solicitous for my safety and health. They have written to me and I enclose an answer which be pleased to envelop and direct to the[m], father, <u>Horatio</u>, at New York and please pay the postage. They have always been kind to me and take great interest in me.

Uncle Peter Scales wrote to me when he saw I was in Mexico. Do write to him and tell him I will write when I have an opportunity to send a letter to him. Now, my father Goodbye. I shall write every chance I get but they occur very rarely. I shall try to do my duty to my God and country and leave the result with Him who will do what is best. My love to all the family.

Yours affectionately,

Theodore

⁙ • ⁙

Laidley's estimate of American losses during the siege of Puebla (September 13, 1847 to October 12, 1847) was very accurate. Eighteen American soldiers died, and fifty more were wounded.[9]

---

[1] K. Jack Bauer, *The Mexican War* (New York: Macmillan, 1974), 270.

[2] Bauer, 295.

[3] Bauer, 301.

[4] Bauer, 307.

[5] Bauer, 308–11.

[6] Richard B. Winders, "Puebla's Forgotten Heroes," *Military History of the West* 24, no. 1 (Spring 1994), 10–12.

[7] Winders, 15–16.

[8] This is the second time within these letters that Laidley has complained of some pre-existing condition, the extent of which remains a mystery.

[9] Richard H. Coolidge, *Statistical Report of the Sickness and Mortality in the Army of the United States compiled from the Records of the Surgeon General's Office; Embracing a Period of Sixteen Years, From January, 1839, to January 1855* (Washington, D.C.: A.O.P. Nicholson, 1856), 615, 619.

letter 15

Laidley's letter of October 18 merely recaps his letter of two days earlier in case that first letter was intercepted by Mexican bandits along the road from Puebla to Veracruz. Obviously it was not.

Puebla, Mexico Oct. 18ᵗʰ 1847

My dear Father

I wrote a letter to you a day or two since but I find I have, now, an opportunity of sending another, and lest the last one may fail to reach your hands I will write a few lines by this opportunity, as most probably this conveyance will reach Vera Cruz before the other and may be get to your hands first.

If it do, it will be of interest to you to know what I have there said at greater length that I have been mercifully spared and protected from all the dangers which have encompassed me, thus far. I know you have been anxiously scanning the papers to hear of me in Mexico [City], but I have had no opportunity of letting you know that I was not there but left behind as part of the garrison of this place—a movement as unexpected as unpleasant, it was only determined on after the Army had begun to leave and it fell to my lot by regular detail so I could not complain.

I have no doubt that it has all happened for the best, that He who knows what is best for us will do for us who trust in his goodness that which will tend most for our happiness.

I was anxious to go to the great city and I still hope I may have that pleasure as I have orders to join the main Army as soon as the Governor of this place says he can spare me. As he will be superceded soon and sent on to join his regiment I hope he will let me go on with him, and not turn me over to his successor, still to form a part of the regular garrison of this place. Though if we are to occupy the country for any length of time I presume I shall be sent to this place, Jalapa or Perote—that the Ordinance officers will instead of being kept at one place at Mexico [City] will be distributed about at the different stations.

At any rate I will try and go on the first opportunity and remain there as long as I can, for you have no idea how much more pleasant it is with regular troops where everything is conducted with some order and regularity. There, in the City, I shall have the advantage of the society of some few pious friends, and a Chaplain, neither of which I have here.

I have seen the Governor's report of the siege. He speaks of all in the most exalted terms, those that were not exposed, as well as those who were exposed to much danger. I am mentioned very highly, but he has spoken of others, who I thought did not deserve it, in such high terms that I do not care much for his commendations—it is so common that it has lost much of its value.

My dear father, your letters are coming in finely. The last mail brought me <u>five</u> and the one before four. I think I must have received nearly all. They are not sent up except when a train is sent and there is not much danger of their being lost— the letters from the states to this country are pretty sure to come safely though they are apt to be a long time in getting here.

We have to send ours, to you, by couriers and expresses which are liable to be cut off. You will not regret having written to me frequently if you knew what a comfort they were to me—how they encourage me and urge me on to do my duty to be faithful in the discharge of my duty to my God and contend against the temptations that surround me. Surrounded as I am by such evil influences I require every assistance to contend against evil examples. I keep pretty much to myself, have no intimates and I believe I have succeeded in gaining the good will and respect of all with whom I have been associated without sacrificing any duty or principle.

Now our siege has terminated many are running into the extreme of intemperance and I fear some of them will meet with the consequences before long—a leave of absence of an indefinite length.

My health is improving, I think, of course I am much better than when I left you, otherwise I could not have performed what I have been called upon.

But the cause of my indisposition is not yet removed, and the consequences of it are rendered lighter in this fine climate. My life, now, is not as active as I would like to have it—we are still confined to very narrow limits not daring to venture far from our troops.

I am in hopes, though, if nothing happens to prevent it, my health may still improve—this climate though it does not agree with all, has, with me, very much. Since the Army left here, more than two months since, we have buried about six hundred men—

to be sure there were left behind here the sick of all the army, but the people of the States have no idea of the amount of sickness and deaths there are here in the Army—arising from imprudence and exposure. I understand Capt. McComas was left very sick in Jalapa, and where Joseph Samuels is I do not know. His company is here, though I have not seen any of them.

I hope my other letter will reach you, for I have there been more particular in the details of our late siege, and the prospects of its getting to you safely has prevented me from giving it over again in this.

We all would be delighted to get back to a civilized land, but when are we? The Army has done wonders in the way of fighting but they cannot make peace. None wish for peace as ardently as the Army.

Give my love to the family and let me hear from you often, write whenever you feel like it, and when you do not do not forget me. Let me always have a place in your prayers as you have in mine.

God help you, my father, Yrs.

Theodore

Colonel Childs did indeed single Laidley out for praise in his report of the siege of Puebla. "Lieutenant Laidley, of the ordnance corps," he wrote, "commanded the 12-pounder, the mountain howitzer, and four rocket batteries at the barricade, and there stationed himself night after night; and, as often as these batteries were opened, it was with effect." The source of Laidley's disappointment, however, is in the sentences immediately following, where Childs singled out other officers even though they had not done much to deserve praise. He commends a cavalry officer, for example, who saw no action but "was at all times ready." Likewise, another officer, "although not attacked, was vigilant."[1]

Elisha W. McComas and Joseph Samuels were, like Laidley, Virginians although not graduates of West Point. Both had been commissioned as captains in the newly created 11th U.S. Infantry Regiment on February 23, 1847. McComas recovered from his illness and was honorably mustered out at the end of the war. Samuels died on December 9, 1847.[2]

---

[1] Report of Col. Thomas Childs, October 13, 1847, in Serial Set 503, Senate Executive Document 1, 30th Congress, 1st session, 474.

[2] Francis Bernard Heitman, *Historical Register and Dictionary of the United States Army, from Its Organization, September 29, 1789, to March 2, 1903* (Washington, D.C.: Government Printing Office, 1903), vol. 2, 658, 858.

letter 16

The arrival of General Lane with reinforcements from Veracruz had broken the Mexican siege of Puebla, but as long as the enemy troops were still in the area they were a danger. General Rea had retired to the vicinity of the town of Atlixco, some twenty to thirty miles southwest of Puebla, and Lane meant to give him no rest. On October 19, a 1500-man contingent, which included some artillery, routed Rea's forces with a minimal loss to the Americans. Next, Lane turned his attention toward another guerrilla base at Tlaxcala, about thirty miles north of Puebla, with similarly satisfying results.

Puebla, Mex, Oct. 24ᵗʰ 1847

My dear Father

A few days since I wrote to you and the troop of horse that was to carry it started, had a pretty severe encounter with the enemy had twelve of their number killed and others wounded

117

were compelled to return. There was a native spy company in our service, headed by the greatest outlaw and robber in Mexico, which is saying a good deal. I have just learned that they are going to start again to-morrow escorted by other troops and there will be a fine chance to send letters and papers. I cannot forego the pleasure, and sit down this Holy day to tell you how often I think of you, especially on every return of this day, and envy you the privileges you enjoy, the privileges of the Gospel.

Knowing that it is a trial that I am now undergoing, I try to make the best use of it, and shutting myself up in my room with my Bible and Prayer Book I try and join in the prayers and praises of the Church which so many thousands are at the same time offering up to Him who hears them all.

He is among the soldiers, but little regard is paid to this Holy day. Many would not know it was Sunday were it not that they do not have to drill—as it is, it is a day of idleness and dissipation.

The Mexicans do not observe it as strictly as it is in the U.S. Their churches are open and many attend and seem very devout, but they do not proclaim it a day of rest and rejoicing by their dress, by shutting their shops, by abstaining from all labor & etc.—their dress is as usual on other days—most of the shops are open as on other days, the people seem to be engaged, bringing articles to Market and other acts of Labor very much as usual. In the morning they ride or walk in the public walks, visit public places of amusements and at night they regularly have their music and dancing which is kept up till a pretty late hour.

I heard a piece of news, yesterday, so good that I feel almost ready to hug the delusive hope that it may be true. A gentleman said (Mexican, I must say) that he had just recd a letter from his brother in Mexico [City], that he wrote that the Mexican Congress had met at some place near the city, that Mr. Trist had been out there and there was a fair prospect of a treaty being concluded in two or three months—if I had not been deceived so often, or if it were any other nation than the Mexican, I would believe it, but as it is, I will believe it when the treaty starts for Washington—its persons would rejoice more than the Army.

I have one word more to say about Gov. Childs report, you, taking the interest of a father, have a right to know what I have been doing and what credit belongs to it. As to people generally I do not care if they do not know. The Gov. in his report calls me an "excellent officer"—so far, very good, and I thank him for his compliment. But when speaking of what I did he slurs it over, and does not speak of my firing as highly as of the others, though I was the only one that he complimented for the accuracy of my firing, whereas he abused the others for not firing better.

Col. [Albert C.] Ramsay [Ramsey] & [Lt.] Col [Samuel W.] Black [of the 1st Pennsylvania Volunteers], both of whom saw all, gave me the highest compliments for the part that I bore in the siege—the former told me that I had performed the most important part of all and the hardest. The latter says that my firing was the only firing that did any good and that mine was done with great skill and accuracy. You would not think this from the Gov's report. That I did do my duties faithfully and with skill, I claim—that my duties were as important as fatiguing and as dangerous as those of any other officer, I also claim—and what I want you to know is that these my claims are admitted by officers and men of the garrison, though the Gov. in his report does not say so.

I am disgusted with the way his report is written, officers who did nothing and whom he abused for worthlessness, in his report are praised for their efficiency and spoken more highly of than others who did their duty and received his commendations.

These Penn. volunteers are trying to make the people of the U.S. believe that the siege of Puebla is the greatest on record; that the deeds of valor performed by them have not been equalled since the days of Napolean. They have established a paper and are heralding their daring exploits to the world, as well as some they did not perform, and anything complimentary to officers of the regular army cannot find admission—for instance at a dinner given to Col. Childs some of us regulars were toasted—but in the paper they do not appear, where others do that were never made at dinner.

The regulars do not act thus. If others do not publish their merits, their exploits they do not do it themselves, and they are ready to give the volunteers the credit they deserve. No wonder the people should think highly of the volunteers when they fill the newspapers with their own stories exaggerated so that they would not be known by those who were participators in their glorious actions.

But the other side of the story is not heard. How they rob houses, steal, sack churches, ruin families, plunder and pillage. No, this is not heard of. But the poor sufferers know and hear it. The outrages they have committed, here, will never be known by people of the U.S. They would not believe it if they did hear of it—But enough.

In two or three weeks, I hope to go on to the city [Mexico City]. I hope I may not be disappointed. The weather is delightful, a succession of fine weather that is not known in the U.S. It is very fine.

We expect a [wagon] train up in ten days when I hope I shall hear from you again. I think there will be trains going down more regularly hereafter than there has been. My health is pretty good.

Give my love to the family. I remain very affectionately

Yours. <u>Theodore</u>

⇻ • ⇺

The "spy company" to which Laidley refers was indeed a band of robbers. Manuel Dominguez headed up this group of brigands. Prior to his employment by the U.S. Army in June 1847, he had regularly stopped travelers along the road to Veracruz and robbed them or offered to sell them safe passage certificates. The size of the spy company soon grew to over a hundred men, and all of them shared the same seedy reputation as their leader. American officers put them to good use, patrolling the roads all the way from Veracruz to Mexico City on the alert for information of use to their employers.[1]

---

[1] A. Brooke Caruso, *The Mexican Spy Company: United States Covert Operations in Mexico, 1845–1848* (Jefferson, North Carolina and London: McFarland and Company, 1991), 152–54.

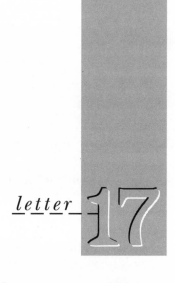

letter 17

Puebla, Mex. Nov. 5ᵗʰ 1847

My dear Father

I have another opportunity of sending you a letter and though I have nothing new or important to communicate still, I cannot let it pass without saying to you that I am well. I also send you a draft on the Quarter Master in New Orleans for two hundred and fifty dollars, which I trust you will have no difficulty in cashing, as the Q. Master is as good as the Mint. I hoped to send more but just at this time, I had to buy a horse, some one having shot mine, a drunken soldier, I believe. Whether he gets over it or not I cannot tell. I still have some hopes.

The train from Mexico brings us for the first time the news of the late battles and it seems that we will never get done hearing of the killed and wounded. Many of the wounded are along, some on crutches, some limping others with only one arm; it is terrible, the destruction of life and the amount of suffering. I knew many of those who fell, some of them intimately, and some fine men who did fair to do well and be useful members of society, were among them.

All of my Corps were actively engaged and were conspicuous for usefulness; they all escaped unhurt, though in some hot places.

The Capt. promised to relieve me for a while and let me visit the City of Mexico; I want to go there to stay; for here I shall be with volunteers and no regulars, which will be any thing but pleasant.

Monday last was a great day with the Mexicans—All-Saints-Day—the shops were mostly closed but few persons were at work; in the afternoon, every one turned out to ride or walk and such an array of beautiful shawls I never saw. It seems indispensible for every one to have an embroidered shawl costing from twenty five to one hundred and fifty—usually of the brightest and most gaudy colors.

It is customary when the Americans are not here, to gamble universally, but this year they did not amuse themselves in that manner, but the plaza was filled with persons of all grades and all costumes. When I went to tea that night I found a table set out and three tall wax candles burning on it—it was loaded with cakes of all kinds, fruits also and a large glass of water—I asked what it meant, the reply was "It is for the dead." It is a custom universal in Mexico. I asked if they thought it would profit the dead, they said the cakes & fruits would not, but the candles would, and as in triumph asked if "it was not dark in purgatory?" The next day is what is called "the day of the dead." All day long the bells were tolling a particular note, and I asked what it meant? "it is for the dead" was the reply. On this day it is customary to visit the Church Yards and take with them all kinds of good things to eat and plenty of Pulque, and get drunk and in the evenings fights and quarrels are plenty and many are killed every year. This is the way they celebrate their great feast days. I do not know that I have stated that I am living with a Mexican family—we do not eat at the same table, but sometimes they give me a real Mexican dinner. And a strange enough affair is it to an American. Their ideas of the culinary art differs very widely from ours. They make great use of red peppers and some of their dishes it is almost impossible for one to taste who is not accustomed to it. Tortillas, a thin, very thin cake of indian meal baked on a hot plate is a very common kind of bread and almost indispensable to a Mexican. I have tasted it but it did not please my palate, and in truth very few of their dishes would please any one, at first trial. Their pulque I like very much and it is a very nutritious and healthful beverage; about as strong as sharp cider or porter—but Mexicans get intoxicated on it very frequently—it is manufactured in great quantities and is the daily drink of almost every Mexican—a cent and a half or "clako" of Mexican coin being sufficient to buy a large glass full—a very good drink.

Nothing certain about my going on to the city yet. From the descriptions of the battles at Mexico I should have been in the midst of it—but I suppose it is all for the best.

Give my love to all

Yours sincerely
<u>Theodore</u>
Write me constantly.

As there were no large scale battles after the siege of Puebla, the news of fighting that Laidley received from Mexico City must have referred to scattered outbreaks of guerrilla activities.

Like Laidley, many soldiers sampled the local cuisine, if only to relieve the boredom of their regular fare. The reactions varied. Some were quite taken with it, like the man who thought that he had tasted "nothing more palatable" than tamales. Others believed that Mexican cooks used entirely too much hot seasoning. An Illinois volunteer officer who admitted subjecting himself to Mexican dinners on more than one occasion just "to be in fashion," suffered nightmares from the highly spiced food. "I eat a few of these," he wrote, "[and] that night dreamed that my throat was the crater of a volcano."[1]

Not everyone who tasted pulque, made from the maguey plant, shared Laidley's evaluation of it as being "healthful and nutritious." The Scottish-born wife of the Spanish ambassador to Mexico a few years before the war recorded her impressions of pulque in a rather different tone than the lieutenant. "On a first impression," she wrote, "it appears to me, that as nectar was the drink of Olympus, we may fairly conjecture that Pluto cultivated the maguey in his dominions." "It is said," she continued, "that when one gets over the first shock, it is very agreeable. The difficulty must consist of getting over it."[2]

---

[1] J. R. McClanahan to his sister, October 25, 1846, McClanahan-Taylor collection, University of North Carolina Library, Chapel Hill, North Carolina; George Rutledge Gibson, *Journal of a Soldier Under Kearny and Doniphan, 1846–1847*, ed. Ralph P. Bieber (Glendale, California: Arthur H. Clarke, 1935, reprint, Philadelphia: Porcupine Press, 1974), 315; Will Wallace to his sister, Helen M. Indson, November 16, 1846, Wallace-Dickey collection, Illinois State Historical Library, Springfield, Illinois.

[2] Frances Calderon de la Barca, *Life in Mexico* (1843, reprint, New York: Dutton, 1970), 43.

By November, fighting between American soldiers and Mexican government forces had virtually ceased, but there were still a number of Mexican guerrilla bands operating along the route from Veracruz to Mexico City. They raided wagon trains, capturing the teamsters and confiscating their cargoes. Their activities were more than a minor irritant to American officials, and some U.S. troops stayed busy tracking down and attacking the outlaw bands.

Early in November, Colonel Francis M. Wynkoop detached a company of mounted Texas Rangers from his garrison at Perote and led it on a raid to the headquarters of a noted guerrilla leader in the area. The operation was almost textbook perfect. The Americans captured all but one of the suspected guerrillas, including the leader, and found that two of their captives were officers of the Mexican army who had previously given their parole not to take up arms against the Americans. Breaking such a parole was a capital offense, and both men faced firing squads later in the month.[1]

General Lane was also busy chasing down guerrillas in the vicinity of Puebla. On a raid into Tlaxcala on the night of November 9–10, his force captured thirteen bandits and a fair number of horses and cattle. The 500-man force had arrived too late, however, to save all twenty-eight of the wagons of a recently captured train. The Mexicans had already burned seven of them. A raid two weeks later into Izucar de Matamoros also yielded significant results. Leading a much smaller force of mounted volunteers from Texas and Louisiana, Lane managed to liberate two dozen American prisoners and seize two cannons, while at the same time killing and wounding quite a number of Mexicans.[2]

Even though anti-guerrilla activity offered excitement to those who participated in it, most American occupation troops in Mexico by this time spent more energy fighting boredom than enemy soldiers.

Puebla, Mex. Dec. 1ˢᵗ 1847

My dear Father

Genl Twiggs is expected to-day from Mexico on his way to Vera Cruz, to take command of that State, which presents us an opportunity of sending off letters, which we readily embrace.

The news from Mexico [City] and in fact of all Mexico you will learn sooner from the papers than from me, and there fore in general, I leave you to get it from that source, confining myself to that more personal, more relating to myself. Communications are not frequent between the different parts of Mexico yet, and we are not informed what was the purport of the despatches that passed here, more than two weeks since, to Genl Scott. Of course we have found conjectures, and doubtless this movement of Genl Twiggs is in conformity to those instructions.

Genl Patterson who is now in a days march from this place, and who will bring us letters from you, and good news, I hope, will remain here and be the Governor of the State of Puebla. Genl Worth, I understand is to go on to Queretaro and take command of that State.

My hopes of going on to the City are pretty well blasted— they were founded on the expectation that the former Governor of the city, Col. Childs, would in obedience to orders, join his regiment in Mexico and the new comer would let me go on—but the Col likes better the position of Governor of this place than at the head of his regiment, and it seems he has succeeded in getting the order countermanded, and he told me but a day or two since that he supposed he and I would have to remain. I suppose it would be impossible for the city of the angels to get along without the presence of two such distinguished individuals. The one is about as necessary as the other, and I can say that there is very little use of an Ordinance officer, here. But great men, I mean high in rank, are fond of having a dozen satellites revolving about them, it increased their own importance, or they think it does; they must have as many Staff officers as they can get, and if they have nothing to do they can accompany the Genl in his rides or walks.

However, I am content to remain here, it is quite a pleasant place and if I had some regular officers for associates, and a chaplain I would be perfectly contented. The climate is better than in the city of Mexico and from what I hear on all sides, the ancient City can well compare with any in the world for iniquity. Any Mexican city is bad enough but the capital excels them all.

I suppose we need not think of getting out of the Country for years to come, I have accordingly gone to work to learn the language and am getting along pretty well—it is very easy, more so than the French, and is the prettiest language I have ever heard, by far. When well spoken, it is very musical, and also expressive. The Mexicans do not speak the pure Spanish, but in some instances quite different—using many provincialisms, and somewhat different pronunciation in many words. In a short time I hope to speak it fluently as well as write and read it.

A few days since I visited the Palace of the late Bishop; I had heard of its fine paintings and library and was glad of an opportunity to witness them. The paintings were certainly beautiful some of them by the Old Masters, others copies—the collection is large and finer far than I ever saw the property of a single individual. The library contains eighteen thousand volumes, in French, Italian, Latin, Spanish, Greek & Hebrew, some few in English. It is estimated to be worth sixty thousand dollars—the gallery of paintings, more. After going round and seeing all these evidences of opulence I asked of the person who was showing us around, if the Bishop were not wealthy? No, he replied, with a shrug of the shoulder, but his predecessor was. I thought they had a different manner of estimating riches from that I was accustomed to. His library, paintings and everything that he owned are to be sold and the proceeds, after defraying his debts, are to go to the poor. He was quite eminent for his learning, friendly to the Americans, and was the same whose hand Gen Worth kissed, when we first arrived here. This was his city palace. At another time I will tell you about his country palace.

Dec. 12th 1847

The above was written expecting Genl Twiggs the next day: you can form some idea of the manner we are hoaxed by false rumors when I tell you the Genl will arrive to-day, some of his troops are already in, and they bring me orders to join the Army in Mexico. I will start in a day or two, with my orders considerably cooled. I like Puebla very well and am not so anxious to go on as I was. Mexico is colder and damper and more expensive and I will not any longer be my own master. But I will again have the great privilege of Christian friends, and attending the worship of God in his Temple. But I fear it will be of short duration, they will send us off to San Luis Potosi or some other place, and I will be worse off than ever, farther from home, unable to hear as regularly as I now do. But there is no use objecting—go I must—and it may prove far better than anticipated.

Genl Patterson's train brought me a letter from you—of September—and Genl Butler's that will be in to-day, I hope will bring me another. They are great comforts to me, and when you are assured that they will come to hand, at some time, I hope you will write more fully and with more confidence.

I have been a little unwell for a few days, a little bilious, but a dose of blue mass has restored me, and I feel better. The old trouble, I do not get over, in this delightful climate, however, I do not suffer so much from its effects. Give my love to the family.

Your affectionate son
<u>Theodore</u>

꘎ • ꘎

Laidley's letter of December 1, shows an interesting range of emotions. On the one hand, it is obvious that he still is eager to press on to Mexico City, but with his chances "pretty well blasted" he has decided that Puebla is not such a bad place after all. It almost seems as if he believes that by putting such words to paper he will ultimately come to believe them himself.

With his hopes of seeing Mexico City dashed, Laidley must rely on the reports of others to form an opinion of life in the nation's capital. This second hand information often included positive comments about the city itself—the architecture, the climate—but contributed to the negative stereotype of the Mexican people already so firmly ingrained into the minds of most American soldiers. A North Carolina volunteer, for example, found the city itself to be quite handsome, but most of the people he saw he categorized as "Low rascally fellows wrapped up in their Blankets and who would murder every soldier they can if they dared." Another man compared the ornate splendor of the various churches he saw to the peasant squalor all around him. "As for their intellectual powers," he wrote of the peasants, "little can be said in their favor. As a general rule I believe our negroes are their superiors in mental abilities."[3]

Lieutenant Laidley was among those men who decided to use part of their spare time to learn the local language. Such knowledge had obvious benefits to an occupying army. For example, it would allow the soldiers to conduct commercial transactions in the market places more easily. It also eased relations between officers and civilian officials with whom they had regular interaction. And there was also a baser motive. Many soldiers found themselves smitten by the beauty of Mexican women, but the lack of an efficient means of communication often blocked their efforts to pursue more intimate relationships. A Kentucky volunteer hinted at this frustration to his brothers when he described his recent attendance at a fandango. He had had a good time with the pretty senoritas, he told them, but "I could enjoy myself as well with them as with the Americans if I understood their language better. I am at a loss what to say to them which causes some uneasiness with the ladies and myself."[4]

Of course, any time that two cultures are thrust into intimate proximity with one another, as when the American soldiers and Mexican civilians came in contact, the language barrier often leads to amusing incidents in spite of the best efforts of all parties. In one instance, an officer of the 1st Illinois Volunteers with a flair for languages did not let his lack of a Spanish vocabulary stand in the way of his attempts at conversation. When attempting to converse with a local woman, for example, he augmented his meager knowledge of her language with much pointing and gesticulating. "When at fault for a word," he wrote in describing one such encounter, "I take an English one & give it a Spanish ending & pronunciation & make a salaam or two. . . . If that don't go, I throw in a word or two of Latin & French, & occasionally a little German, & conclude with 'Senora' or 'Senorita.'" Unfortunately, his performance gave his listener a higher opinion of his linguistic abilities than was truly warranted, and she immediately "let loose a torrent of Castillian on me, & I stand & look knowing, & say 'Si Sinorita' when I've no more idea of what they are saying than if Moses was talking to me in his native tongue." Not all Americans took such a light-hearted approach to such incidents. Another man, searching the chaparral for a strayed horse, came upon a Mexican and asked him, in a badly fractured mix of English and Spanish, if he had seen the animal. The Mexican replied, "No entiende, señor." "Don't understand!" muttered the exasperated American. *"Why the d____d fool don't know his own language!"*[5]

Laidley again complains about his health in this letter, although this time he gives us a little more of a hint as to the nature of his discomfort. His feeling "a little bilious" may very well be a touch of jaundice or even yellow fever. The "blue mass" to which he referred, and that seemed to have helped him feel better, was calomel, or mercury chloride. Doctors regularly prescribed this mixture of mercury, powdered liquorice, powdered rose leaves, and honey to alleviate the symptoms of constipation that yellow fever patients so often experienced.[6]

[1] K. Jack Bauer, *The Mexican War* (New York: Macmillan, 1974), 334.

[2] Bauer, 334.

[3] J. L. P. Cantwell to Benjamin Lucas, October 27, 1847, John L. P. Cantwell papers, University of North Carolina Library, Chapel Hill, North Carolina; Robert Hagan diary, University of Texas Archives, Austin, Texas.

[4] Thomas T. Summers to his brothers, November 15, 1846, Thomas T. Summers papers, Filson Club, Louisville, Kentucky.

[5] William Seaton Henry, *Campaign Sketches of the War with Mexico* (New York: Harper and Brothers; 1847, reprint, New York: Arno Press, 1973), 157–58.

[6] Gordon Dammann, *Pictorial Encyclopedia of Civil War Medical Instruments and Equipment* (Missoula, Montana: Pictorial Histories Publishing Company, 1983), 62.

City of Mexico Jan. 11ᵗʰ 1848

My dear Father

The expectation of an expedition being dispached to San Louis Potosi very soon brought me to the Great City where I arrived the 20ᵗʰ of last month.

The expedition did not get off as was expected, for want of an adequate force, and I have thus had an opportunity of seeing something of the Capital, whilst waiting for reinforcements to arrive.

We were not disturbed at all in our march to this place, though we had a very long train of wagons, some four miles or more in length, and passed through some very strong holds, where a few resolute men could do great injury to a large force, and cut to pieces a train no better protected than our own was. The pass of Rio Frio defended properly would stop a force four times as large as the defending ones. It is the strongest that we have come across yet. It is very high and cold, being over 10,000 ft. above the level of the sea; I thought I should freeze the night we stopped there—water froze of great thickness and the frost assumed the appearance of snow, it was so thick, our thin tents were but poor protection against it. We had plenty of wood and built up our camp fires, and I have never seen so pretty sight, during the campaign, as our camp presented after night, with the numerous fires blazing over the valley of more than a mile square.

The finest sight, that of the valley of Mexico just as you begin to descend we lost as the clouds lying below us shut it out completely. I hear every one who came along with the Army at first speak of it as being the grandest sight they ever saw, and I can well conceive it to be such. At this season of the year, when everything seems parched, for the want of water it is not so pretty, but we could see the extent of it embracing at one glance the whole valley of Mexico, surrounded on all sides by the immense chain of mountains, its surface here and there dotted with lakes and small volcanic, conical-shaped hills.

The main road to the City leads by El Peñon that they had so strongly fortified, and sad work would it have been if we had attempted to force a way through.

I had no conception that the city was so well fortified on all sides as it really is, and their field works are beautiful, skillfully and scientifically executed, so that if the other departments had done their duties as faithfully as did the Engineers, we should not have been at this time in the city.

Water, deep ditches filled with water, breast works on all sides, nothing but the greatest cowardice can account for their poor defence.

Of course a city of the great antiquity of this presents many points of interest—The first thing that I gratified my curiosity on was the battle fields—I rode over the whole with persons who were able to describe the whole affair, tell me the positions held and the manner of attack so that I got a perfect idea of the whole affair—and corrected many erroneous ones that I had formed from reading the newspaper accounts of the battles. The success of our arms was truly great and astonishing and is only to be attributed to the hand of an overruling Providence who does as seemest best in his own eyes.

On my arrival I found the Ordnance officers comfortably established in [Maj.] Genl [Gabriel] Valencia's house, where I took up my quarters with them. I have a comfortable room, looking out on the public walk or park, with a carpet, settee, chairs &c and a bust of Washington. In the court yard is a fountain and orange trees loaded with golden fruit, flower pots with flowers blooming and blossoming. One of our greatest luxuries is a fire place the only one, but one or two, in the city, and as the houses are so open they are very pleasant of a morning and evening.

We have a good market, plenty of wild ducks, and vegetables and fruits, though we have to pay for everything most extravagently. I walked through the market on New Year's day and I could not realize that it was the depth of winter. There were green peas, radishes, potatoes, tomatoes, cabbage, Cauliflower, bulb [?] turnips, squashes, oranges, bananas, may apples, chirimayer[?] (which very much resembles in taste the paw-paw, only improved), and every thing that you could imagine, the day was fine, bright sun and cloudless sky, persons selecting the shady side of the street, it was difficult for me, accustomed to the extreme north, to believe that this was really winter.

I went to the palace to call on the [U.S. Military] Governor [Brig.] Genl [Persifor F.] Smith, in reaching his apartments which are those of Santa Anna's, we passed through a fine room a kind of ante room, where was seen a large full length picture of Genl Washington, which had taken place of that of Iturbide, when [our] troops took possession.

In the reception room of the palace, a very handsome room we have the service every sunday, twice. It makes a long pretty chapel; one end is raised several steps, which forms the desk and altar—elegant chairs of crimson velvet seats for the congregation to sit upon, and a fine brussels carpet to kneel upon.

It is a great privilege and I esteem it highly, that of once more kneeling at this altar, and of entering in the prayers and praises of His Holy Church. I think we might have a few more chaplains sent out, that every post of any size might not be deprived of these advantages, of which they stand so much in need. There are a good many who attend from the highest General to the lowest private. All like and speak highly of the chaplain, the fighting parson, as he is frequently called. His sharing the dangers of battle, reproaching the skulking and encouraging the others, has drawn him close to them all, and he is liked by them for it.

The future is all uncertain—what is to be done? and when is this to end? Is our Government going to prosecute the war with vigor, or are we still to fight with forlorn hopes? These are questions in the mouths of all, without any one being able to solve them. The continual hard fighting without gaining anything, volunteers getting all the glory without the fighting, seeing citizens rise above them without merit or anything to recommend them has disgust[ed] all and the officers do not hesitate to say, they have seen enough let the Volunteers do the rest, let them go to themselves and do it their own way and see how they will come out.

My health is very good. Give my love to all.

Yours affectionately
Theodore

Finally, Lieutenant Laidley has reached Mexico City. Once again, he has reunited with other ordnance officers, and once again he is able to attend the church services of Reverend McCarty.

The relative peace that settled over Mexico City soon gave rise to some high level squabbling within the American army. It allowed time for tender egos to reflect upon real or imagined slights during the campaign. Some of the officers involved undoubtedly realized that with the war now virtually at an end there would be no more opportunity to win personal glory. The careers of regular army officers were very dependent on their having won brevets for gallantry, and volunteer officers likewise counted on attaining martial honors to advance their post-war careers in business or politics.

General Worth had a long list of complaints, stretching back to when Taylor's army was still camped at Corpus Christi before the war began. The first problem arose over a dispute about relative rank between himself and David E. Twiggs. Both held the permanent rank of colonel, although Twiggs outranked Worth because his promotion to that rank bore an earlier date than Worth's. Twiggs therefore claimed the right to be second in command to General Taylor. Worth also laid claim to this honor based upon his brevet rank of brigadier general. The argument between the two finally reached the point that President Polk, in his constitutional capacity as commander in chief of the armed forces, intervened. He upheld Twiggs's claim, causing Worth to resign from the service in a huff, although he quickly returned to duty as soon as the war began.

Worth next got crosswise with his old friend General Scott. In spite of President Polk's earlier ruling, Worth believed that he should have had the honor of leading the advance out of Veracruz toward Puebla, but Scott instead gave Twiggs the lead. Then, several months later, Worth attempted to shift the blame for the heavy American losses at Molino del Rey onto Scott, and he also believed that the commanding general had not adequately credited his contributions to the victory at Churubusco.

Brevet Colonel James Duncan, a regular army artillery officer who had become quite friendly with both Generals Pillow and Worth, also began to feel slighted by Scott. He had written a letter to a friend in which he apparently claimed for himself and General Worth much of the credit for having selected General Scott's route through the valley of Mexico and up to the capital city. The friend then caused the letter to be published in a newspaper, after *much* editing and rewriting. The finished version seemed to suggest that Scott improperly claimed the credit for selecting the proper route in his official report, and that he had neglected to mention the contributions of Worth and Duncan.

General Pillow was the third person to enter the fray with the commanding general. Pillow owed his high rank to nothing more than the fact that he had been President Polk's close friend back in Tennessee. His lack of formal military training and experience did not, however, stand in the way of his using the war as a stepping stone to the future. He shamelessly used the media to claim complete credit for the American victory at Contreras. His method was not uncommon. Soldiers, usually volunteers, often wrote letters to their hometown newspapers describing battles in which they had taken part. Many of these self congratulatory, and often pseudonymous, letters contained battle accounts that were so heavily embellished as to bear little resemblance to the official reports which usually came out later. Army regulations had forbidden such communications ever since 1825, but for some reason this particular stricture was not included in the most recent regulations, those of 1841. Such letters finally became so flagrant as to prompt President Polk, on January 28, 1847, to forbid all such privately written accounts until a month after the conclusion of any given campaign or battle.

The New Orleans *Delta*, however, published such a letter on September 10, 1847, and, as was common in those days, several other papers picked it up and republished it. This letter, published over the signature "Leonidas," was an amazing piece of puffery. It compared Pillow's military prowess quite favorably with that of Napoleon Bonaparte, and claimed for him all the credit for planning and carrying into execution the attack on Mexican forces near Contreras. "Nothing could have been better planned than this battle," Leonidas declared, and claimed that General Scott was "so perfectly well pleased with it" that he could find no reason to change any part of it. Leonidas likened General Pillow to Napoleon and hinted that only the timidity of General Scott prevented Pillow's men from capturing Mexico City that very day.[1]

After reading the "Leonidas" letter General Scott quite understandably assumed that either Pillow or one of his subordinates within the army had written it. It was certainly not the only such letter to appear in American newspapers, but it was one of the more blatant. Rather than point an accusing finger at just Pillow, Scott issued a general order to the army on November 12, 1847, reminding the men that writing such accounts was forbidden. The entire situation degenerated rapidly after that.

Instead of General Pillow making some sort of explanatory response, General Worth now stepped in. He believed that Scott's general order had been a backhanded attack on *his* honor, and when he could not obtain satisfaction from his commander he complained directly to the President, accusing Scott of conduct unbecoming an officer. Meanwhile, Colonel Duncan owned up to having written at least one of the many offending letters, so Scott brought charges against him on November 18, 1847. General Pillow became directly involved when he wrote directly to Secretary of War William Marcy asking him for a hearing with regard to the "Leonidas" letter. This violation of the chain of command gave Scott the opportunity of filing formal charges against Pillow.

As this intraservice wrangling continued, President Polk stepped in and on January 13, 1848, ordered a formal court of inquiry to be held to look into all of the charges and counter-charges. Though the court did not begin formal proceedings until three months later, the army was abuzz with rumors as soon as word reached Mexico that there was to be such a hearing. At the same time that the President ordered the court to convene he also took the opportunity of relieving General Scott of command of the troops in Mexico and replacing him with Major General William O. Butler.

Of course the bickering among the American high command was not the only subject of interest in the Mexican capital after the virtual cessation of hostilities. There still remained the problem of working out an acceptable peace treaty, but talks aimed at accomplishing this were not progressing very rapidly. President Polk was convinced that sterner steps needed to be taken, and he also believed that Nicholas Trist was too willing to entertain Mexican counterproposals that the president found patently unacceptable. He therefore instructed Secretary of State James Buchanan to order Trist to abandon further talks and return to Washington.

Trist, meanwhile, seems to have been doing his level best to come up with a legitimate peace treaty. One of the big difficulties that he faced was finding someone within the Mexican government who had the authority and the inclination to sit down and talk. Mexico was rent by political feuds and uprisings. It was virtually political suicide for any government official to consent to the loss of New Mexico and California, as Trist was demanding. In fact, at one point the following tongue-in-cheek notice appeared in an American newspaper in Mexico City:

> Wanted immediately—A government in Mexico qualified to do general housework, sign documents, or at least make its mark. Such a government, which can furnish satisfactory recommendations from its last place may procure a situation by addressing post paid James K. Polk, Washington, or by applying personally to General Winfield Scott, Hall of the Montezumas, second door below the grand plaza. N.B. No Protestant need apply.[2]

Progress began to be made when a new government took over in Mexico at the end of October. Foreign Minister Manuel de la Peña y Peña seemed willing to reopen negotiations and, in fact, named four commissioners to work with Trist. Then, on November 16, Trist received his recall notice from Buchanan. He let Peña know, through unofficial channels, of the change in his instructions and intimated that a workable peace agreement might still be attained if the Mexican commissioners and congress worked quickly. A week later, with no measurable progress to report, Trist began making plans to return to the United States by December 4 or 5, depending upon when the next wagon train left for Veracruz.

While Trist waited for transportation to the coast, he faced much pressure to remain and work with the Mexican commissioners in spite of his orders to return. Perhaps the most cogent argument was that unless Trist was able to sign a treaty the American demands on Mexico might increase to the point that it would become impossible to reach an acceptable, workable agreement. Trist decided, therefore, to stay on in Mexico City in violation of his orders. "Knowing it to be the very last chance," he wrote, "and impressed with the dreadful consequences to our country which cannot fail to attend the loss of that chance I will make a treaty, if it can be done," on the basis of his original instructions.[3] Having made this decision, Trist then sat down and wrote out a sixty-five-page letter to Secretary of State Buchanan justifying his decision.

The political turmoil within Mexico still prevented any substantive peace talks from taking place for the rest of December, but private talks finally began on January 2, 1848. As is usually the case in such situations, each side viewed the other's opening demands as being totally unrealistic. When Foreign Minister Peña became interim president on January 8, he told Trist that the original American offer of fifteen million dollars was simply not enough. He must have thirty million. Trist refused.

City of Mexico, Feb. 11th 18478

My dear Father

The British courier leaves to-morrow and the speed with which he goes and consequently much shorter time my letter will be on the road induces me to accept the offer of a friend to forward a letter by him, though we are told a larger train will leave <u>next</u> <u>week</u>, for Vera Cruz.

The news of the Court of Inquiry has just reached us and has calmed our fears that Genl Scott was to be recalled which would be the greatest misfortune that could possibly happen to the Army.

This court is going to be a long and tedious affair [and?] will bring to light enough to settle Genl Pillow, whilst, I think, it will not hurt Genl Scott, further than perhaps as he is concerned with the <u>presidency</u>, and I am inclined to believe that this is the bottom of the whole of it.

We have had great talk about peace and you have doubtless, heard of the treaty that has been sent on, but we have learned not to trust on a Mexican, for if White man is mighty uncertain, Mexicans are <u>more</u> so, and as the treaty has yet to pass the ordeal of passing the Congress here, though many think it will, still there is place for some doubt and we cannot make any calculations about leaving yet awhile.

My chief, Capt. Huger, has been ordered home, much to my regret, he is such an accomplished officer and Gentleman that I dislike to part with him, well knowing that his place cannot be filled. All movements further into the interior are postponed till we hear from Wash. and know what will be done about peace, so I am still here waiting till an advance movement is ordered, which I am to accompany. My teeth have been troubling me again, cold feet as ever; one side of my face, now, differs much in its fair proportions from the other—I don't see when it is to end.

My latest date from you is the last of Nov. I knew you would suffer much from suspense, though I was in hopes you would be relieved much sooner. But do not trouble yourself about such things; any unwelcome news would very soon reach you, much

sooner than good—"ill news flies fast"—and you may save yourself a great deal of pain by not anticipating it before it comes.
We are to have a mail next week when I hope to hear from you,
and I shall write again in a few days—so Good bye, till then.

Yours affectionately <u>Theodore</u>

---

[1] Serial Set 510, Senate Executive Document 65, 30th Congress, 1st session, 388.

[2] Mexico City *North American,* January 29, 1848, in Robert Louis Bodson, "A Description of the United States Occupation of Mexico as Reported by American Newspapers Published in Vera Cruz, Puebla, and Mexico City, September 14, 1847, to July
31, 1848" Ed.D. diss., Ball State University, 1971, 233.

[3] K. Jack Bauer, *The Mexican War* (New York: Macmillan, 1974), 382.

letter 21

General Butler took formal command of the American military forces in central Mexico on February 19, 1848, but Scott stayed on in Mexico City waiting for the court of inquiry to meet. The officers making up the court met in Mexico City from April 13 to April 22. They found no reason to believe that General Pillow had written the infamous "Leonidas" letter, so Pillow, feeling exonerated, then withdrew his complaints against Scott. Scott left the Mexican capital the day after the conclusion of the hearings and returned to New York.

Peace negotiations were still glacially slow, and by the end of January even Nicholas Trist's patience had begun to wear thin. He informed the Mexican commissioners on January 29 that unless they could reach an agreement by February 1 he was going to break off the talks altogether and, presumably, return to the United States. Two days later the Mexican commissioners accepted a draft treaty and sent it to President Peña for his approval.

The main points of the document called for Mexico to recognize the loss of Texas, whose border was permanently set at the Rio Grande River. The United States was also to gain New

Mexico and California in return for a payment of fifteen million dollars. The various claims for damages which American citizens had lodged against the Mexican government before the war, approximately three million, were now to be paid by the U.S. government. The U.S. would not, however, receive transit rights across the Isthmus of Tehuantepec because they had already been granted to British interests.

There was reluctance on the part of some Mexican officials to sign the treaty. Among the arguments against a hasty approval were those advanced by Manuel Crescencio Rejon, a liberal from Yucatan. He maintained that the treaty had been drawn up in secret, which violated Mexican law, that it had not been made public, and that government officials were now being asked to approve it without time for serious debate. Others, on the other hand, recognized that Mexico was not being forced to cede all the lands that were then occupied by American troops. Had that been the case, after all, it would have meant giving up such important cities as Monterrey, Saltillo, Veracruz, and even Mexico City itself. "The treaty," this faction reasoned, "may be more properly called a treaty of recovery rather than one of alienation."[1] Probably concluding that this document was the best he was likely to get, Peña authorized its acceptance, and it was duly signed on February 2, 1848, at Guadalupe Hidalgo. Both countries now had four months in which to ratify the document.

City of Mexico
March 22ᵈ 1848

My dear Father

Our mail conveniences are beginning to improve considerably; we got another one on monday which brought me yours
of Feby 15ᵗʰ. I believe we are to have two mails, hereafter regularly per month and the same number will likewise depart for
Vera Cruz, which will be a vast improvement over the former
arrangements. But there is no reason why we should not have
regular mails, we certainly have been put to enough inconve-
nience, by the want of them, and if we are to remain here, I
donot think our Government has done so much for us that it
cannot afford to let us hear from our friends at regular intervals.

I am sorry to hear that your health is still so feeble; I was in
hopes that it was better as you had not mentioned it for sometime.

Your mention that many of the inhabitants of Guyandotte
had joined the Church gave me much satisfaction, though my
own observation has taught me that such times of excitement
are always succeeded by corresponding ones of apathy in which
many fall away, still we may hope that some will remain constant and remember their good resolutions made in such times.

Though we have the services of the church regularly, twice
on Sunday, the attendance is very small, and has somewhat dis-
heartened our chaplain. The truth is we are in a very bad moral
atmosphere, and surrounded by so many temptations and no
public opinion to frown down the many irregularities of life
religion is but little thought of, and its restraints but little heeded.

Sunday is the great day for horse-racing, balls, theatres, and
pleasure excursions of all kinds, and our people, principally,

outsiders, hangers-on, teamsters, Quartermaster's men, etc display a wonderful aptness in adopting the manners and customs of the people where the[y] find themselves, I think they rather outstrip the natives on many of the roads to vice. 'Tis no wonder that the Mexicans should form a low opinion of us as a people, since they have the dregs of our own country to form their opinion from. Most of those who come out here seem to have left all conscience of right and wrong at home and commit actions without shame that they would blush to do when under the restraints of society at home. A long, long time will it be before we get over the ill consequences of this war; its influence shall be felt when the cause shall have been forgotten. May we soon be delivered from it, and returned to the healthier restraints of a Christian society, be delivered from the miasma that seems to affect most all who inhale it.

As yet we have no news of treaty—it has been looked for several days, but has not yet made its appearance. There are but few who are of the opinion that we will get out this spring, before the yellow fever, and the rest seem to have made up their minds to stay till fall and think themselves fortunate if they get out then. Preparations are being made in the Quartermaster's department to move the sick to Jalapa, and mending wagons etc to take us to the sea coast if required.

Personally, I am not so anxious as very many to get away. I am lo[a]th to leave this delightful climate, knowing that it must be better for me than the changeable one of the north and if I am ever to get well, I stand a much better chance of it here than at home, and in many respects this is a more pleasant post than any of our Arsenals. And as long as we have a chaplain, and several pious comrades as I have in Lt. C[harles] P. Stone of my corps my most constant companion and Lt. R[alph] W. Kirkham of 6th Infy. a classmate of mine and old friend, and others, I have not so great a desire to get back to the states to go over again the miserable hours I have spent, principally, from ill health.[2] Of course I should like to visit you all, but if I returned I could stay but a short time before I would have to leave again to go to some station. I am desirous to go back home much improved in health and am not anxious to return before.

The principal matter of interest now in the city is the Court of Inquiry. Genl Worth has withdrawn his charges against Genl Scott and Genl Scott withdrew his against Genl Pillow and Col. Duncan. Genl [P]illow insisted too strongly on having his investigated, and the court is now proceeding to investigate them. The first witness proved very clearly that Genl [P]illow did have the "Leonidas" letter written and published. The other evidence will be pretty much of the same kind; the charges, I think, will be clearly proved, and he[,] the said [P]illow[,] will be killed as dead in the states as he is in the army. His conduct has been of the most unblushing character, and if the Pres[ident]. had ordered a Court as he was in duty bound to try him, he, Genl [P]illow would have been dismissed the service, I think there is no doubt. Direct falsehood can too easily be proved on him. The Army generally is with Genl Scott. They knew that there is no one of the Generals that can at all compare with him; as an officer said the other day "Genl Scott's little finger is more of a general than all of the other generals put together. Genl Smith is next to him, and those of more reputation in the States have very little claims at all to be called generals.["]

My trip to the mines was of service to me, I have felt better since I returned. I should like to take such a trip every week, if for no other purpose than the exercise. I got several specimens of ores that I would like to get to you, but I suppose I will have to wait till I can come myself.

There are several places of interest near here that I intend to visit if we remain during the summer, for as yet we have seen little of the country, only that portion lying directly on the main road from Vera Cruz to this place. Though hostilities have nominally ceased, still we have to exercise the same precautions in going from one place to another as before. The guerrilla parties are as numerous and kill and rob the same as ever. This puts a great hindrance to travelling and prevents us from visiting where we would otherwise go.

The weather is very pleasant cloudless skies, warm in the sun but cool in the shade. Looking over the register of weather for this month I find the Thermometer at 2 o'clock ranges from 62 to 72—The weather "fair, fair, fair" all the way through, no rain, and but little wind.

I have procured a map of the city and its environs, embracing the battle fields, a better one, more accurate than any you have seen, which I send to you. It will assist in understanding the various reports, of the different battles, though cannot fully comprehend the difficulties our army encountered without seeing the ground itself. For all the hard work done by our officers, all the dangers seen, the brilliant deeds of gallantry performed by officers and men, I understand, they are to get <u>nothing</u> not even the empty honor of a brevet commission. I do think it is too hard, too mean. When was an army ever treated so—not given even the promotion caused by deaths in battle, but some one who was not in the battles at all poked in to fill the vacancies—Whose only recommendation is that he is a <u>drunken</u> democrat. It is too bad. Fortunately it does not effect me, personally.

Give my love to all. I hope this may find you in better health.

Yours very affectionately,
<u>Theodore</u>

⫯ ● ⫯

Laidley had definitely settled in to a regimen of activity in Mexico City that was much more to his liking. Surrounded by friends and former classmates, with an acceptable preacher thrown into the mix, the young officer indeed was in no hurry to go home. Nor was the press of official business too great, since he had plenty of time to go sightseeing in the area.

---

[1] Richard Griswold del Castillo, *The Treaty of Guadalupe Hidalgo: A Legacy of Conflict* (Norman and London: University of Oklahoma Press, 1990), 50.

[2] Kirkham's account of his experiences during the Mexican War may be found in *The Mexican War Journal and Letters of Ralph W. Kirkham*, ed. Robert Ryal Miller, (College Station: Texas A & M University Press, 1991).

letter 22

City of Mexico, April 6ᵗʰ 1848

My dear Father

I have been to-day on a very pleasant and interesting little trip, over the same ground, the same route that Cortez took on being driven out of the city on the "noche triste." With a small party we started at eight, and soon passed the spot pointed out as "Alvardo leap," where formerly was a small stream, but is now spanned by an arch or culvert. About three miles to the west of the city lies Tacuba [Tacubaya?] where Cortez on the same night reached the dry land and rested his troops till day. Though then a flourishing place, it is all now in ruins, an old Church and a house or two only remaining, built by the spaniards, is all of the village at this time. A large cedar tree is pointed out by tradition as marking the spot where Cortez slept after the toils and danger of that melancholy night: It is an enormous tree, being more than fifty feet in circumference and from other marks of antiquity I can well conceive that it might have been a large sized tree in the times of Cortez three and a quarter centuries since.

154

In Tacuba there are other vestiges of the ancient inhabitants. A large mound built of sun dried bricks still remains though of no great height. It has been dug into and lines have been thrown up. It covers a large space and was doubtless in former times applied to the same purposes as Cholula and others of the kind. Afterwards, we pursued the route that Cortez took the succeeding morning, up to the highlands and halted where he took up his position on a commanding hill to recruit his worn out forces preparatory to retreating to Tlascala. At this place the Spaniards built a Church and dedicated it to "Our lady of Remedies," one of the characters of the Virgin Mary, which still remains in good order, far too fresh looking to be so old.

There is in the church an image of the Virgin said to have been brought over by Cortez himself, which was shown to us.

In the Church are several rough pictures of remedies worked by "our lady" on application to her, besides many offerings stuck up on the wall of persons who have experienced relief from "our lady of Remedies."

From this place we had a fine view of the valley; the city showed its spires and domes, beyond it stretched the lake of Tezcuco [Texcoco]: The green fields lay stretched out before us studded with trees in full foliage, whilst surrounding the whole, like a frame to a picture, was the vast chain of mountains, many more than usual covered with snow.

It must have been a terrible time for Cortez when he stood where we were then standing under such different circumstances—Surrounded on all sides by so numerous and desperate an enemy, a mere handful and far from any succouring help. Had our opposing force had the courage, and perseverance of their ancestors we should never have been standing there contemplating the trials of Cortez.

But Cortez had no newly made Generals and no valiant volunteers to fight his cause and of course he failed on this occasion.

The Court of Inquiry still goes on, developing facts that you little thought, I presume. The Army generally are pleased that the trial is going on as it will set many matters right and give credit where credit is due and strip others of their stolen honors. It is thought it will close its settings here in another week beside this when it will adjourn for the United States.

News has finally reached us that the senate, after a long delay which cost the Government some millions of dollars, has ratified the treaty with some amendments, and Mr. Sevier will be here some time or other with the treaty in hand—which will bring it in the sickly season before we can get out. To be sure loosing a few thousand more from sickness passing through Vera Cruz in the summer is of no importance to the Government, [page torn] it ought to be avoided if possible which it would, if all despatch had been used. Genl Butler says he thinks we will all get out this summer, that the Mexican Congress will work more rapidly than ours and we will immediately be put in motion for the sea coast. The sick are to be moved to Jalapa next week, but they are so numerous that it is no slight undertaking, and will retard our motions very much when once we get the order to move.

About one fourth of the whole army is sick; sometime since it was a greater proportion. In an army of some sixteen thousand men, the number of sick is quite considerable and requires a deal of transportation to move them. We are waiting with some degree of impatience for the treaty—we have heard of its passage nearly a week.

City of Mexico, April 7<u>th</u> 1848

The doctors have been starving me again and reduced me to a skeleton almost again. But I still keep stirring and keep along without giving up. Col Velasquez is here and talking so that I cannot write any more.

I send you <u>two</u> checks for one hundred dollars each, which please acknowledge as soon as you can.

The two last mails brought nothing for me; I hope, however, that nothing is the matter, and that the next mail will bring me a letter.

Give my love to all the family.

Your affectionate son
<u>Theodore</u>

City of Mexico, May 13th 1848

My dear Father

I let the last mail go off without sending you a letter, so I will write by the British Courier who leaves to-morrow, a friend having kindly promised to have it forwarded for me.

We are in such a state of uncertainty as to whether we shall have peace or war, whether we shall leave immediately or remain till fall in the event of peace, that I have no desire to write till the thing is definitely settled.

You have doubtless seen from the papers that Congress has assembled, both houses organized, and the President's very sensible message. But you have also seen that [Maj. Gen. Mariano] Paredes is trying to get up a revolution in Aguascaliente, and if you are as well acquainted with these people as those who have been in their country for sometime, and seen them more closely, you will grant that a peace is by no means certain yet. One day we have news from Querétaro that the peace prospects are very bright, that they are going to take up the treaty and pass it immediately, and we are to be on our way home in a few days; perhaps the very next day, we hear there are no hopes of peace, at all, that some general is getting up a pronunciamento against the Government, and the members of Congress have sworn to leave their seats when the Treaty is brought up before them.

And so it goes from day to day, so that we have learned to pay no attention to reports of either kind and are passively waiting till the 2$^{\underline{d}}$ of June when we shall <u>know</u> which way we move in advance or retreat.

It is a very common question, now, on meeting, to ask "How is peace stode [today?]" and usually with a smile, as much as to say it is not at all important which way you answer the question.

The high officers, generally, are quite confident that the treaty will be ratified, though even this has no weight with the most of us, for the good reason that they have invariably, been humbugged, heretofore, have always believed we would have peace, and still there is none. But if you ask anyone under the rank of Colonel, "Are we going to have peace?" the answer is a shrug of the shoulder with "Quien sabe"—"Who knows?"

Now that Genl Scott has left, the desire of the Army is tenfold for peace. You ought to have seen the parting of the General from some of his officers, when he left the city. He has manifested great delicacy in leaving, and the course he is to pursue going home.

He says that now whilst laboring under the Executive displeasure it is not proper for him to have any honors bestowed upon him, and he carefully abstains from all <u>glorification</u>. He kept it a perfect secret the time he was going to start, and it was not known till late in the evening that he was to leave next morning. Some officers who heard of his intention asked permission to call on him, but he returned answer that he was too much occupied.

The next morning he got in a carriage, early, and left without any escort, but he pretty soon had one, of officers, who had learned his leavings. There were perhaps thirty officers who rode out with him a short distance, when he requested Genl Patterson to take them back, not to let them go any further with him. Previous to leaving him, he stopped his carriage, the officers dismounted and going up to the carriage, their hats off, gave him a hearty shake of the hand, with a kind wish for a safe and speedy return to his family; some with the tears rolling down their bronzed cheeks, and those whose tears refused to come to their relief, so agitated that they could not say a word, but a convulsive shake of the hand told of their feelings within, on bidding adieu to their chief who had led from victory to victory, and who never before, when dangers thickened and all looked black and desponding had showed himself unnerved by the circumstances surrounding him—and then, too, he was leaving them, under the displeasure of the Government, returning from his brilliant victories not [to] be crowned by a grateful people and receive their enthusiastic applause for his noble, meritorious and brilliant achievements, but to the contrary, he is recalled from the scene of his fame, in all the disgrace that it was possible to heap on him.

Then, too, those officers felt that should we have more active operations, we should no longer have him to look up to and feel that confidence that the army always has felt, under his command.

The General was much affected, and I should rather had his feelings on that occasion than those who have caused him to leave the Army under such circumstances. A proud moment must it have been for him to see the attachment of his officers, their devotion to him when they had nothing to expect in return.

Had he let it be known that he was going, he would have had hundreds of officers to escort him on the road instead of thirty.

With the strong feeling that the officers have for him there is no telling how far he might not carry them if he should make the effort.

I see from the papers that Virginia has been doing a whole-sale business in presenting her gallant sons a reward for their distinguished services. She has forgotten that by making them so common they will lose their value. Any one who was born in Va. and whose name appears in the report it matters not what they did, how little, they are to have a sword. A great many were much a[stonished? (page torn)] to find themselves Virginians, with a sword presented them. Since they have taken away the honor, it is to be hoped they will make up in the beauty of the present.

We are expecting the Brevets by the next mail, and then we shall have more grumbling and swearing than for the last six months. It is expected they will be given as favors to political friends and the meritorious who have no friends will go a beg-ging for any reward of service; when they see others who have done nothing but exert their influence at Washington outstrip-ping them and rising to high commands. I have seen enough of Military glory, and know of what queer stuff it is made not to learn me to think but little of it, and to be little anxious to gain it, certainly not to place my thoughts and affections upon it.

Ours is the last country in the world for a man to expect to rise to military distinction, by careful attention to his profes-sion or by any merit he may possess as an officer, but let him go and edit a radical newspaper, turn demagogue and he is certain of his reward. These are subjects I wish I never thought upon, for it does no good, but they are constantly thrown before our eyes that we must see and feel how we are treated. We are called to associate with as gentlemen, men who have not the least pretensions to the name. There are some two or three who have just been under trial for burglary and murder, and we expect to see them executed for their crimes—<u>officers</u> of the American Army!! hung for burglary!

'Tis no longer an honor to belong to the army—A carte blanche to the best society, a certificate of being a gentleman or a scholar.

My health is just so, so—About as poor and weak as ever. And though I have been following, strictly, the prescriptions of the doctors for a long time, still no change for the better. They say patience, patience but it is not very encouraging to wait and wait and see no change for the better.

The last mail brought me no letter from you, though it was the regular mail two weeks after the last. Give my love to all.

Yours affectionately
<u>Theodore</u>

In spite of the many false rumors flying about, Laidley's information on the progress of the treaty was fairly accurate. Article XI of that document indeed required that Mexico and the United States exchange ratifications within four months of the treaty's signing. Since the date of the signing was February 2, 1848, ratifications were required by June 2.[1]

Laidley's high opinion of General Scott never seems to have wavered. Indeed, his heartfelt description of the general's departure for the United States indicates that he was probably one of that group of officers who bid him a fond farewell.

With his favorite general removed from the scene and the war drawing to an official close, Laidley found time to grouse about perceived injustices that he observed. His home state of Virginia came in for a share of his indignation. The fact that Virginia chose to bestow a presentation sword upon each of the company officers of its single volunteer regiment was not all that unusual. States often honored their returning warriors in some such fashion. Daniel H. Hill, a classmate of Laidley at the Military Academy, received a very ornate presentation sword from his home state of South Carolina, although not until almost ten years after the war. The awards that Laidley complained of had been authorized by the Virginia legislature back in February 1847, at which time most of the members of the Virginia Volunteers had not even arrived in Mexico yet. Most, indeed, had not even left Virginia. Adding more to Laidley's foul mood was the fact that when the Virginia volunteers did finally reach Mexico they were too late to participate in *any* battles and thereby lay legitimate claim to such martial honors as the state bestowed upon them. But what may have irritated Laidley as much as anything about the whole affair was that in choosing to thus honor her native sons Virginia completely ignored the contributions of its native-born officers in the regular army— like Laidley himself.[2]

Laidley was also pessimistic about his chances for promotion, even though he had performed well in combat. Even a brevet, or honorary, promotion seemed too much to hope for when Laidley wrote this letter. He was unaware that he had, in fact, already earned two brevet promotions. His performance at Cerro Gordo resulted in his name being put forward for a brevet promotion to captain. Likewise his bravery during the siege of Puebla was recognized with the rank of brevet major. Had he known of these honors when he wrote this letter its tone would surely have been a little less morose.[3]

The crime to which Laidley refers was a burglary and murder that occurred in Mexico City on April 5, 1848. Several American soldiers *and officers* broke into a gambling hall late at night, and when the owner appeared one of them shot him in the head and killed him. Such crimes were, unfortunately, not rare among the occupying army, but the participation of officers was. Ultimately the trial board sentenced seven men to pay the ultimate price for their crime. They were to be "hanged by the neck until they are dead, dead, dead." General Butler, after approving the sentences, had a change of heart with regard to the enlisted men and spared them. Lieutenants Isaac Hare and Benjamin F. Dutton of the 2nd Pennsylvania Volunteers, Lieutenant Bryant P. Tilden of the 2nd U.S. Infantry, and a gambler by the name of Lafferty still remained scheduled to face the hangman on May 25. By late May, however, the American evacuation of Mexico was underway and Butler may have believed that hanging these men to set an example for others would now be academic, so he also freed them.[4]

What undoubtedly rankled Laidley as much as having army *officers* besmirch the reputation of the U.S. Army was the fact that Tilden was an officer of the Regular Army and a West Point graduate in the Class of 1840. In fact, it is likely that Laidley knew him personally since their times at the Academy overlapped.

---

[1] Richard Griswold del Castillo, *The Treaty of Guadalupe Hidalgo: A Legacy of Conflict* (Norman and London: University of Oklahoma Press, 1990), 199.

[2] Jack Allen Meyer, *South Carolina in the Mexican War: A History of the Palmetto Regiment of Volunteers 1846–1917* (Columbia: The South Carolina Department of Archives and History, 1996), 169; H. W. Flournoy, compiler, *Calendar of Virginia State Papers and Other Manuscripts from January 1, 1836 to April 15, 1869; Preserved in the Capitol at Richmond* (Richmond: 1893), vol. 11, 19.

[3] Francis Bernard Heitman, *Historical Register and Dictionary of the United States Army, from Its Organization, September 29, 1789, to March 2, 1903* (Washington, D.C.: Government Printing Office, 1903), vol. 2, 611; George W. Cullum, *Biographical Register of the Officers and Graduates of the U.S. Military Academy at West Point, N.Y. from its*

Establishment, in 1802, to 1890 with the Early History of the United States Military Academy (Boston and New York: Houghton Mifflin, 1891), vol. 2, 116.

⁴ Ulysses S. Grant to Julia Dent, May 27, 1848 in Ulysses S. Grant, *The Papers of Ulysses S. Grant, Vol. 1, 1837–1861*, ed. John Y. Simon (Carbondale, Illinois: Southern Illinois University Press, 1967), 159; Daniel Runyon to his father, April 22, 1848 and May 20, 1848, Runyon Family papers, Filson Club, Louisville, Kentucky; George W. Hartman, *A Private's Own Journal: Giving An Account of the Battles in Mexico Under Gen'l. Scott* (Greencastle, Pennsylvania: E. Robinson, 1849), 23, 25; Allan Peskin, ed., *Volunteers: The Mexican War Journals of Private Richard Coulter and Sergeant Thomas Barclay, Company E, Second Pennsylvania Infantry* (Kent, Ohio: Kent State University Press, 1991), 282–83, 298–99.

Epilogue

The American evacuation of Mexico City began on May 27, 1848, even before the two governments exchanged ratified copies of the peace treaty. After General Worth's division moved out from the Grand Plaza on June 12 and headed back toward Veracruz, the capital city was entirely free of the force that had occupied it for the last nine months. As each contingent of American troops neared the coastal fever zone, it halted at Jalapa until the transport ships had arrived at Veracruz and were ready to begin boarding for the short trip across the Gulf of Mexico to the United States. A short march down to the coast, through the city, and onto the ships reduced the time of exposure to the dreaded yellow fever. It would be a shame to have survived all the vicious fighting in central Mexico only to be felled by disease while on the way back home. The last of Worth's men sailed on July 15, leaving only a small number of men to arrange for the transportation of the last of the supplies. Finally, on August 2, the military occupation of Mexico ended.

After returning from Mexico, Brevet Major Laidley received orders back to Watervliet Arsenal, where he was once again to serve as an assistant ordnance officer. This assignment gave the young officer a chance to resume friendships among the arsenal staff as well as the local civilians. One such relationship, with Horatio Averell's daughter Jane, soon became much more than casual, for on October 2, 1848, Theodore Laidley married Jane Averell.[1]

The newlyweds did not have much time to settle down because before the year was out, the War Department transferred Laidley to Fort Monroe, Virginia. It was back to Watervliet in 1852, and then on to the command of the North Carolina Arsenal from 1854 to 1858. He then took a few years off to compile a new ordnance manual, which he completed in September 1861.

By that time, of course, the United States was again at war—this time with itself. Laidley, a captain as of July 1, 1856, served as a gunpowder inspector for a couple of months after the outbreak of hostilities until he took over command of the Frankford Arsenal on February 1, 1862. He remained at this post—being promoted to major on June 1, 1863—until August 19, 1864. He spent the next five weeks as an inspector of ordnance and then took command of Springfield Armory, the country's premiere armsmaking facility, on October 27, 1864.

The war was winding down by the time Major Laidley arrived at Springfield, and much had been learned during the fighting. First and foremost, perhaps, from the point of view of the common infantryman, was the need for a faster firing rifle. The weapons used by most of the troops on both sides of the war had barely evolved at all from those used in Mexico in the last war. They still required loading from the muzzle end, although the use of percussion caps had supplanted the flintlock ignition system. The rifled barrels and cylindro-conoidal bullets made these weapons much more accurate than those used at Cerro Gordo and other Mexican battlefields, but the rate of fire was still about the same. An experienced shooter could load, aim, and fire his rifle only about three or four times per minute, and this is where improvement seemed most important.

Major Laidley, therefore, chaired a board early in 1865, to select a replacement for the venerable .58 caliber Springfield rifle—a replacement that would load from the breech end instead of the muzzle. He called the board to order on January 5, and asked that the first order of business be to determine whether the soon-to-be-adopted weapon should fire internally primed cartridges, or whether the board would also consider weapons that used separate percussion caps. There were several weapons on the market, such as Joslyns and Spencers, that used the self-primed cartridges. Both of these weapons had also seen rather extensive use in the hands of Union cavalry during the war and had turned in creditable performances. The board voted quickly, and unanimously, not to consider any rifles that required separate priming caps.

Even with that limiting parameter in place the board received over the next three months some sixty-five different samples of arms that their inventors hoped would suit the needs of the army, and thereby generate large contracts. Among the hopefuls were many companies, such as Remington and Starr, with established reputations in the firearms field. There were also a number of entries from less well known, and less successful inventors. Among the latter class were Major Laidley himself, who collaborated with a Mr. M. Y. Chick to produce a carbine which they submitted for the board's approval.

The testing was fairly rigorous in order to determine how well a weapon might be expected to perform in the hands of troops on campaign. One of the first tests, for example, called for purposely overloading each entry and then firing, to test the strength of the breech mechanism itself. Obviously if this vital part of the weapon failed in service the unfortunate soldier would be left with nothing but a wooden and iron club in his hands. Many of the weapons—including the Laidley-Chick model—failed the breech strength tests and were thereby eliminated. Each gun was submerged in water for a time and then fired to see if there was any detrimental effect. The testers performed rapid fire tests to check each particular design's stamina. More entries fell out when they were unable to hold up under repeated rapid fire.

By early April, as the war drew to a close, there was suddenly much less urgency to find a new weapon, and the board ceased its deliberations after recommending two new weapons systems.

The War Department, instead of adopting either one of the recommendations, did nothing for almost a year, and then convened another trial board to continue testing. This board, which did not include Major Laidley, recommended five different systems for more extensive trials, and the army ultimately adopted a system that merely modified the existing Springfield rifle and was much cheaper to produce than any of its competitors.[2]

Although not destined to lead troops into battle as many of his West Point classmates would do, Major Laidley's dedication to his calling was rewarded by two brevet promotions—to lieutenant colonel and to colonel—on March 13, 1865.

Laidley left Springfield on May 3, 1866, to take up the command of the New York Arsenal. Within about a month he found himself a member of an ordnance board called to examine a new wrought-iron cannon design that the U.S. Navy was considering. He spent October and November as a member of another board attempting to locate a suitable site near New York City for a powder depot. In addition to such usual duties, he also sat on an examination board in March 1867 to determine which ordnance officers were deserving of promotion. That same month saw his own promotion to lieutenant colonel. His tenure at the New York Arsenal ended on April 1, 1871, with a transfer to the Watertown Arsenal in Massachusetts.

Colonel Laidley quickly immersed himself in his work, barely taking time to familiarize himself with his new surroundings. In June he sat on a board considering the purchase of huge fifteen-inch guns, and this was only a foretaste of the kind of work that would more and more make up his professional duties. Other committees he served on while assigned to Watertown dealt with such things as modified navy gun carriages, a plan proposed by his old classmate Col. James Benton to move heavy guns more efficiently and protect the gunners, the manufacture of fifteen-inch Rodman cannons at the South Boston foundry, the methods of ordnance manufacture employed by various European armies, the use of water power at the Rock Island Arsenal, and the examination of a cart proposed for use by the cavalry.

Laidley earned the eagles of a full colonel on April 14, 1875, and two years later undertook to prepare a marksmanship manual for the army. The result, *A Course of Instruction in Rifle Firing*, was published in 1879, and led almost immediately to controversy. Second Lieutenant Edward S. Farrow, not yet three years out of West Point, had also written a book on marksmanship, apparently unbeknownst to Laidley, and offered it to the Secretary of War in early 1879. Farrow's book was well received. A board of officers meeting in Washington reviewed it favorably, and General of the Army William T. Sherman also endorsed its adoption by the army. This show of support undoubtedly concerned Laidley, and he must have felt some betrayal. After all, he had written his manual on instructions from the army, and it now appeared that the free lance effort by Lieutenant Farrow would overshadow his work. Happily for Colonel Laidley, however, the Secretary of War overruled the previous recommendations and approved his manual for adoption by the army.[3]

The Secretary of War's favorable ruling did not end the controversy over Laidley's *Course of Instruction in Rifle Firing*. Colonel George Wingate, Inspector of Rifle Practice for the State of New York, had written a similar work in 1872 called *Manual for Target Practice*. The civilian National Rifle Association had endorsed Wingate's text, but it lost out to Laidley in its bid for army adoption. Wingate then accused the colonel of having pirated material from his book in violation of his copyright. Laidley fired back with both barrels, publishing a pamphlet in which he refuted each of Wingate's accusations one by one. He even pointed out that Wingate himself had taken material from Laidley's 1861 *Ordnance Manual*. Perhaps it was this last point, and the fear of a countersuit, that laid the matter to rest, as it does not appear to have reached the courts.[4] Still the quarrels surrounding the marksmanship manual had taken a toll.

On December 4, 1882, after having served over forty years, Colonel Laidley voluntarily retired from the U.S. Army. He and his wife took up residence at the Glenham Hotel in New York City where they could be near their only child, Elizabeth, who was married to the Reverend H. H. Oberly, rector of Christ Church. Laidley remained very active in his church and spent a fair amount of time ministering to the incarcerated and visiting the patients in Bellevue Hospital.

After three years of such active retirement his strength began to fail him. Perhaps it was due to whatever had caused his complaints of ill health back in the 1840s. Maybe it was simply due to advanced age. At any rate, he decided to visit a milder climate to see if that would have a beneficial effect on his health, so he and his wife left for Florida. While passing through the town of Palatka, about fifty miles southwest of St. Augustine, he suffered a sudden decline. He knew the end was near, but even then he thought of others rather than himself. He wanted to be buried at West Point, but he knew that the necessary arrangements and transportation might be difficult for his wife so he told her, "Do not take me North unless you wish very much to do so." Then, on Sunday night, April 4, 1886, Theodore Laidley died.

His widow, much as Laidley had anticipated, was either unable or at least not ready to deal with the logistics of shipping his body back to West Point for burial, and had him buried in Palatka Cemetery on April 6. His remains were reinterred at the West Point Cemetery on December 22, 1886.[5]

[1] John G. Butler, "Theodore T. S. Laidley," *Seventeenth Annual Reunion of the Association of the Graduates of the United States Military Academy at West Point, New York* (East Saginaw, Michigan: 1886), 104.

[2] Andrew F. Lustyik, *Civil War Carbines: From Service to Sentiment* (Aledo, Illinois: World-Wide Gun Report, 1962), 38–41, 44–48.

[3] Douglas C. McChristian, *An Army of Marksmen: The Development of United States Army Marksmanship in the 19th Century* (Fort Colllins, Colorado: The Old Army Press, 1981), 41.

[4] McChristian, 24–26.

[5] Butler, 109–10.

References

PRIMARY SOURCES

Unpublished

Burns, Archibald. Journal in the Duke University Library, Durham, North Carolina.

Campbell, John. Letters in the University of Virginia Library, Charlottesville, Virginia.

Cantwell, J. L. P. Letters in the John L. P. Cantwell Papers in the University of North Carolina Library, Chapel Hill, North Carolina.

Edwards, Henry. Journal in the Indiana Historical Society Library, Indianapolis, Indiana.

Fincher, John W. Journal in the Atlanta Historical Society Library, Atlanta, Georgia.

Hill, Daniel H. Diary in the University of North Carolina Library, Chapel Hill, North Carolina.

Lowe, John Williamson. Letters in the Dayton and Montgomery County Library, Dayton, Ohio.

McClanahan, J. R. Letters in the McClanahan–Taylor Collection in the University of North Carolina Library, Chapel Hill, North Carolina.

Moore, Sydenham. Journal in the Alabama State Archives, Montgomery, Alabama.

Runyon, Daniel. Letters in the Runyon Family Papers in the Filson Club Library, Louisville, Kentucky.

Smith, Franklin. Journal in the Mississippi Department of Archives and History, Jackson, Mississippi.

Stapp, Wyatt B. Letters at the Filson Club, Louisville, Kentucky.

Summers, Thomas T. Letters in the Filson Club Library, Louisville, Kentucky.

Towner, T. H. Letters in the Benjamin Towner papers in the Duke University Library, Durham, North Carolina.

Wallace, Will. Letters in the Wallace–Dickey collection in the Illinois State Historical Library, Springfield, Illinois.

Books

Anderson, Robert. *An Artillery Officer in the Mexican War 1846–7.* Edited by Eba Anderson Lawton. New York and London: G. P. Putnam's Sons, 1911.

Ballentine, George. *Autobiography of an English Soldier in the United States Army.* New York: Stringer and Townshend, 1853.

Calderon de la Barca, Frances. *Life in Mexico.* 1843, reprint, New York: Dutton, 1970.

Callan, John F., ed. *The Military Laws of the United States Relating to the Army,*
    Volunteers, Militia, and to Bounty Lands and Pensions from the Foundation of the
    Government to the Year 1863. Philadelphia: George W. Childs, 1863.

Coolidge, Richard, comp. *Statistical Report of the Sickness and Mortality in the Army of*
    the United States compiled from the Records of the Surgeon General's Office; Embracing
    a Period of Sixteen Years, From January, 1839, to January 1855. Washington, D.C.:
    A.O.P. Nicholson, 1856.

Flournoy, H. W., comp. *Calendar of Virginia State Papers and Other Manuscripts from*
    January 1, 1836 to April 15, 1869; Preserved in the Capitol at Richmond. Vol. 11.
    Richmond, 1893.

Forman, Sidney, ed. *Cadet Life Before the Mexican War.* West Point, New York: United
    States Military Academy Library, 1945.

Gibson, George Rutledge. *Journal of a Soldier Under Kearny and Doniphan, 1846–*
    1847. Edited by Ralph P. Bieber, Glendale, California: Arthur H. Clarke, 1935,
    reprint, Philadelphia: Porcupine Press, 1974.

Grant, Ulysses S. *The Papers of Ulysses S. Grant.* Edited by John Y. Simon. Carbon-
    dale, Illinois: Southern Illinois University Press, 1967.

_____. *Personal Memoirs of U.S. Grant.* 2 vols. New York: Charles L. Webster and
    Co., 1885–86.

Hartman, George W. *A Private's Own Journal: Giving An Account of the Battles in*
    Mexico Under Gen'l. Scott. Greencastle, Pennsylvnania: E. Robinson, 1849.

Henry, William Seaton. *Campaign Sketches of the War with Mexico.* New York: Harper
    and Brothers, 1847, reprint, New York: Arno Press, 1973.

Kirkham, Ralph W. *The Mexican War Journal and Letters of Ralph W. Kirkham.* Edited
    by Robert Ryal Miller. College Station, Texas: Texas A & M University Press,
    1991.

McAfee, Ward and J. Cordell Robinson, eds. *Origins of the Mexican War: A Documen-*
    tary Source Book. 2 vols. Salisbury, N.C.: Documentary Publications, 1982.

Meade, George G. *The Life and Letters of George Gordon Meade.* 2 vols. New York:
    Scribner's Sons, 1913.

Perry, Oran, comp. *Indiana in the Mexican War.* Indianapolis: Wm. B. Burford,
    1908.

Peskin, Allan, ed. *Volunteers: The Mexican War Journals of Private Richard Coulter and*
    Sergeant Thomas Barclay, Company E, Second Pennsylvania Infantry. Kent, Ohio:
    Kent State University Press, 1991.

Register of the Officers and Cadets of the U.S. Military Academy. (June 1839).

Register of the Officers and Cadets of the U.S. Military Academy. (1840).

Register of the Officers and Cadets of the U.S. Military Academy. (1841).

Articles

Barton, E. H. "Means of Preserving Health at Vera Cruz." *The Boston Medical and*
    Surgical Journal 36, no. 24 (1847): 484.

Butler, John G. "Theodore T. S. Laidley." In *Seventeenth Annual Reunion of the Association of the Graduates of the United States Military Academy at West Point, New York*, 98–112. East Saginaw, Michigan: 1886.

H. [D. H. Hill]. "The Battles of the Rio Grande." *Southern Quarterly Review* New Series, 2, no. 4 (November 1850): 427–63.

Laidley, Theodore T. S. "Breech–Loading Musket." *United States Service Magazine* 3 (January 1865): 60–67.

Nunnelee, S. F. "Alabama in Mexico War." *Alabama Historical Quarterly* 19 (1957): 413–33.

Porter, John B. "Medical and Surgical Notes of Campaigns in the War with Mexico, during the Years 1845, 1846, 1847, and 1848." *The American Journal of the Medical Sciences* 23 (January 1852): 13–37; 24 (July 1852): 13–30; 25 (January 1853): 25–42; 26 (October 1853): 297–333; 35 (April 1858): 347–52.

Tidball, John C. "Getting Through West Point: The Cadet Memoirs of John C. Tidball, Class of 1848." Edited by James L. Morrison, Jr. *Civil War History* 26, no. 4 (December 1980): 304–25.

SECONDARY SOURCES

Unpublished

Bodson, Robert Louis. "A Description of the United States Occupation of Mexico as Reported by American Newspapers Published in Vera Cruz, Puebla, and Mexico City, September 14, 1847, to July 31, 1848." Ed.D. diss., Ball State University, 1971.

Morrison, James Lunsford, Jr. "The United States Military Academy, 1833–1866: Years of Progress and Turmoil." Ph.D. diss., Columbia University, 1970.

Books

Ambrose, Stephen E. *Duty, Honor, Country: A History of West Point*. Baltimore: Johns Hopkins University Press, 1966.

Baker, W. A. and Tre Tryckare. *The Engine Powered Vessel: From Paddle-Wheeler to Nuclear Ship*. New York: Grosset and Dunlap, 1965.

Barker, Eugene C. *The Life of Stephen F. Austin: Founder of Texas, 1793–1836*. Austin and London: University of Texas Press, 1926.

Bauer, K. Jack. *Surfboats and Horse Marines: U.S. Naval Operations in the Mexican War, 1846–1848*. Annapolis, Maryland: United States Naval Institute Press, 1969.

———. *The Mexican War: 1846–1848*. New York: Macmillan, 1974.

Caruso, A. Brooke. *The Mexican Spy Company: United States Covert Operations in Mexico, 1845–1848*. Jefferson, NC and London: McFarland and Co., 1991.

Castillo, Richard Griswold del. *The Treaty of Guadalupe Hidalgo: A Legacy of Conflict*. Norman and London: University of Oklahoma Press, 1990.

Corder, Jim W. *Hunting Lieutenant Chadbourne.* Athens: University of Georgia Press, 1993.

Cullum, George W. *Biographical Register of the Officers and Graduates of the U.S. Military Academy at West Point, New York Since Its Establishment in 1802.* Edited by Wirt Robinson. Supplementary Vol. VI–A. Saginaw, Michigan: Seemann and Peters, 1920.

Dammann, Gordon. *Pictorial Encyclopedia of Civil War Medical Instruments and Equipment.* Missoula, Montana: Pictorial Histories Publishing Company, 1983.

Green, Constance McLaughlin, Harry C. Thomson, and Peter C. Roots. *The Ordnance Department: Planning Munitions for War.* Washington, D.C.: Office of the Chief of Military History, Department of the Army, 1955.

Heitman, Francis Bernard. *Historical Register and Dictionary of the United States Army, from Its Organization, September 29, 1789, to March 2, 1903.* Washington, D.C.: Government Printing Office, 1903.

Johannsen, Robert W. *To the Halls of the Montezumas: The Mexican War in the American Imagination.* New York: Oxford University Press, 1985.

Lustyik, Andrew F. *Civil War Carbines: From Service to Sentiment.* Aledo, Illinois: World-Wide Gun Report, 1962.

McCaffrey, James M. *Army of Manifest Destiny: The American Soldier in the Mexican War, 1846–1848.* New York: New York University Press, 1992.

McChristian, Douglas C. *An Army of Marksmen: The Development of United States Army Marksmanship in the 19th Century.* Fort Collins, Colorado: The Old Army Press, 1981.

Meyer, Jack Allen. *South Carolina in the Mexican War: A History of the Palmetto Regiment of Volunteers, 1846–1917.* Columbia: The South Carolina Department of Archives and History, 1996.

Nevin, David. *The Mexican War.* Alexandria, Virginia: Time-Life Books, 1978.

Smith, Justin H. *The War With Mexico.* 2 vols. New York: Macmillan, 1919; reprint, Gloucester, Mass.: Peter Smith, 1963.

Stern, Philip Van Doren. *Robert E. Lee: The Man and the Soldier.* New York: Bonanza Books, 1963.

Vandiver, Frank E. *Ploughshares into Swords: Josiah Gorgas and Confederate Ordnance.* Austin: University of Texas Press, 1952; reprint 1977.

Warner, Ezra J. *Generals in Gray: Lives of the Confederate Commanders.* Baton Rouge: Louisiana State University Press, 1959.

Weems, John Edward. *To Conquer a Peace: The War Between the United States and Mexico.* Garden City, New York: Doubleday, 1974.

Articles

Duncan, Louis C. "Medical History of General Scott's Campaign to the City of Mexico, 1847." *Military Surgeon* 47, no. 4 (1920): 76–104.

James, Joseph B. "Life at West Point One Hundred Years Ago." *Mississippi Valley Historical Review* 31 (1944–45): 21–40.

McCaffrey, James M., ed. "America's First D-Day: The Veracruz Landing of 1847." *Military History of the West* 25, no. 1 (Spring 1995): 51–68.

Wallace, George Selden. "Laidley." In *Cabell County Annals and Families*. Richmond: Garrett and Massie, 1935.

Winders, Richard B. "Puebla's Forgotten Heroes." *Military History of the West* 24, no. 1 (Spring 1994): 1–23.

Microfilm

National Archives Microfilm Publication 688, *U.S. Military Academy Cadet Application Papers, 1805–1866.*

Index